This is number 80
of a signed, leather-bound, limited edition
of 500 copies of

Grays of Westminster®
Exclusively... Nikon

The Legend and The Legacy

GILLIAN GREENWOOD

Gillian Greenwood

Grays

GRAYS OF WESTMINSTER · LONDON

40 CHURTON STREET

The Legend and The Legacy

40

The Legend and The Legacy

GILLIAN GREENWOOD

To my daughter Anna

Published by Grays of Westminster
40 Churton Street, London, SW1V 2LP, England
info@graysofwestminster.co.uk | www.graysofwestminster.co.uk

ISBN 978-0-9934221-0-2
A C.I.P. catalogue record for this book is available from the British Library.

Designed by Jesse Wilson
www.beyondmedia.co

Printed by L & S Printing, Worthing, West Sussex

CONTENTS

SPECIAL THANKS

I am profoundly grateful to Gray Levett, Uri Zakay and the staff of Grays of Westminster for the assistance they have provided for this project. I would also like to thank Jesse Wilson for his outstanding artistic input, as well as Harry Ricketts for his considerable expertise in bringing the project together.

ACKNOWLEDGEMENTS

Ronny Adsetts, Scott Andrews, Heather Angel, Nigel Atherton, Tami Bahat, Geoffrey & Rona Baker, Alison Batchelor, the late Julie Batcock, Tim Bates, Michael Bond OBE., Agnes Bondier, Stefano Barozzi, Jim Brandenburg, Rachel Bridgen, Kate Bush, Clive Carpenter, Annie Cahill, Mike Clarke, the late Pat Clarke, The Commodore, Adrian Cochrane, Derek Cooke, Garry Coward-Williams, Cressida Elias, Alex Croft, Daniel Croft, Nikolas Croft, Becky Danese, Damien Demolder, Michael Doven, Sarah Eicker, Michael Eleftheriades, Emilija Ellen, Felix Felix, Bruce Fleming, John Ford, Mark Fury, Tony Frewin, Lawrie Garland, Mark Gibson, Tara Gibson, Yasmin Gibson, Jeremy Gilbert, Tetsuro Goto, Malcolm Granger, Karen Hall, Anna & Phil Harbour, Tabitha Hardy, Manuel Harlan, Gemma Harris, Andrew Hewson, Stephen & Fay Howard, Steve & Debbie Hughes, Tony Hurst, Neville Hartle, Bellamy Hunt, Toru Iwaoka, Peter Jepsen, Keith Johnson, Yusaku Kamekura, Mimi Katz, Emma Kellingray, Richard Kirkwood, Konstantin Kochkin, Ani Kowal, Bron Kowal, Tad Kowal, Toni Kowal, John Krish, Stanley Kubrick, Gray Levett, the late Susie Levett, Daniel Lezano, Richard Long, Nestor and Alexia Marie Lopez, Neil Lucas, Dr Mike Maloney OBE, Linda Markley, Hedley Marks, Cassie Marsden, the late Sir Simon Marsden, Toshiyuki Masai, Elaine Mathieson, Heather McGlone, Joe McNally, Pablo Monteagudo, Dr. P.C. Ng, Robert Noel The Lancaster Herald, Caroline Nolan, Lauren Nolan, Andreja Obadic, Kazuhiro Okano, Tristan Oliver, Liz Ostermann, Kridon Panteli, Chris Pearce, Christian Peterson, Moose Peterson, Sharon Peterson, Barbara Piercey, Harry Ricketts Hon. FRPS., the late Geoff Rimmer, Andrew Roast, Katrin Ruckert, Robert Sanger, Valeria Santostasi, Raffi Silvanian, Martin Shann, Dan Sherman, Andrew Skirrow, Brian Slater, Sofia Slavova, Esther Sonneveld Laveau, Bryan Spark, Simon Stafford, John & Nellie Steadman, Paul Stillman, David Suchet CBE., Hidehiko Tanaka, Belinda Tapp, Floris & Kumi Van Der Mueren, Eniko Varadi, Fabrizio Vaccaro, Kazuo Ushida, John Walshe, Andrew Main Wilson, Simon Weir, Chris Weston, Janet Williamson, Robin Williamson, Stephen J. Willis, Tracey Winskill, Jesse Wilson, John Wood, Richard Young, Susan Young, Maia Zakay, Jake Zakay, Uri Zakay, Zoe Zakay

BIBLIOGRAPHY

James Dowsing, *Guide to Pimlico: London's Stucco Wonderland*
Adam Stout, *Pimlico: Deep Well of Glee 1997*
Edward Walford, *Old London: Belgravia, Chelsea & Kensington 1989*

PRESS

"

GRAYS OF WESTMINSTER AND NIKON REPRESENT A TIMELESS PARTNERSHIP AND I AM HONOURED TO BE ABLE TO CELEBRATE THEIR 30TH ANNIVERSARY AND TO BE A PART OF THEIR JOURNEY THROUGH HISTORY.

"

FOREWORD

by the President of the Nikon Corporation, Japan

As I stepped through the doors at Grays of Westminster for the first time, I knew I had arrived somewhere special.

After receiving a warm welcome from all the staff and the eponymous Gray Levett himself, I was led downstairs, where I was greeted by an incredible selection of Nikon past and present. The range of new and second-hand kit and vintage Nikon on display was awe-inspiring. The time, dedication and care that had been taken to curate such a spectacle was overwhelmingly evident.

Grays of Westminster is an establishment that is held in high esteem by Nikon and I felt a deep honour to have the true 'Grays' experience' that so many of our customers enjoy. The unique combination of exclusive support for the Nikon brand, coupled with unparalleled product knowledge, makes a pilgrimage to Grays of Westminster an unmissable experience for any Nikon enthusiast who visits London. *The answer's 'Yes'; what's the question?* is a philosophy deeply embedded in the very core of Grays of Westminster. No request is too obscure, too challenging or too perplexing for the highly knowledgeable staff, who are always on hand to help and ready to impart their Nikon wisdom.

With their 30th anniversary now upon us, we can look back and reflect on the incredible journey that Grays of Westminster has taken, from humble beginnings to paragons of quality and service within the photographic industry. Testament to this, is the Coat of Arms that was granted to Grays of Westminster in 2014, the first ever for a camera shop and an unquestionable stamp of approval for their consistently brilliant service.

The motto beneath the iconic shield on the Coat of Arms reads "Lead in order to serve", which reflects the way in which the business has been run over the years, with Gray Levett's personal dedication and leadership. The heart of Nikon's philosophy is "Trustworthiness and Creativity" and I strongly believe that it is this powerful combination of these two distinct but complimentary philosophies that makes Grays of Westminster unique.

Grays of Westminster and Nikon represent a timeless partnership and I am honoured to be able to celebrate their 30th anniversary and to be a part of their journey through history. Grays is and will continue to be a valued friend and we cannot thank them enough for their loyalty, diligence and service to the photographic industry and to Nikon. ■

Kazuo Ushida 牛田一雄

Kazuo Ushida
President
Representative Director
Nikon Corporation

EXITS AND ENTRANCES

The door opened grudgingly, juddering and straining against the rusty key, as if reluctant to reveal its secrets. They entered the building like forensic scientists at a crime scene, trying to avoid touching anything around them. There was an overwhelming smell of dankness, a sense of foreboding, the feeling of decay. The paintwork was scratched and stained; the ancient linoleum flooring had disintegrated into chipped, matted patches, spattered with dark spots. In the far corner was a stack of old magazines and musty paperwork, the yellowing receipts *Whites Barbers* just visible through the gloom. Mirrors, sinks and hard-back chairs from the 1940s and 1950s lay cracked and broken on the floor under a covering of dust, dirt and cobwebs of hair. It was as if the place had been turned over by the ghosts of unhappy customers or unhinged vandals from the twilight zone who had accidentally found their way to the wrong street, the wrong shop, and through the wrong time-warp.

"Why are we here?"

"This old barber shop seems to fit the bill."

"Fit the bill for what?"

"New premises."

"For whom?"

Gray Levett hesitated. *"For Grays of Westminster. The address has a nice ring to it: 40 Churton Street, SW1. I think it might just work."*.

HEATHER ANGEL

Heather Angel has been at the forefront of nature photography in Britain for four decades and is acclaimed worldwide as an award-winning photographer. Her images range from intricate macro studies to action wildlife shots and combine scientific accuracy with a strong pictorial appeal. Heather is a past President of the Royal Photographic Society and a Visiting Professor at Nottingham University.

Always an enthusiastic communicator, Heather passes on her expertise via her workshops, exhibitions, articles and blogs, with her 60th book published in Autumn 2015.

http://heatherangelphotography.co.uk

"When Gray Levett founded Grays of Westminster three decades ago, it started as a modest mail order company. Today it is Europe's largest Nikon dealer. Located in Pimlico in central London, the multi-award winning shop is unlike any other photographic retail outlet; it is unique. Any Nikon devotee that steps inside discovers an Aladdin's cave. By specialising in a single brand, Grays of Westminster stocks all the latest camera models, lenses and accessories in addition to the most extensive range of second-hand Nikon equipment. No used item appears for sale unless it is in mint or excellent condition and has been thoroughly checked.

"However, regardless of the stock held, it will not fly off the shelves unless backed up by an enthusiastic and knowledgeable staff. That is precisely where Grays of Westminster scores with a service that is simply the best. Back in 2012, I discovered my Nikon PB4 bellows, purchased in 1982, were no longer usable because the black paint was flaking off the unit. The current PB6 bellows does not have the shift and tilt facility on the front extension, so the only option was a renovation. Toni Kowal at Grays received the old bellows on a Monday. Two days later, a courier delivered the refurbished bellows. That is what I call service!

"I have little doubt, if I was working on a remote island and had a catastrophic disaster with some equipment, I would awake one morning, open my tent flap to see a canoe heading towards me carrying the distinctive Grays of Westminster bag!

"Congratulations to Gray Levett and all the staff at Grays of Westminster on your 30th anniversary and for maintaining your unrivalled standard of supreme excellence, by graciously serving all who visit Pimlico – whether amateur enthusiasts or established professionals."

– Professor Heather Angel
MSc, DSc (Hon), FBIPP, FRPS

CHAPTER 1
LEGACY

In 2015 we commemorated the 800th anniversary of the signing of the Magna Carta at Runnymede. The spirit of those times, the epic imprint of those events, lives on, not only in the imagery of scripted parchment or painted canvas, but in the narrative of the legacy left behind.

In its most essential form, a legacy is an endowment, an inheritance, a gift bequeathed. It can also be the infusing of wisdom and the imparting of ideals, the intuitive words written by a poet or philosopher that stays with you for the rest of your life, the clarity of vision touched on by any creative endeavour in a multitude of different fields.

In 2015 Grays of Westminster celebrated their thirtieth anniversary, the company conceived of by Gray Levett in 1985.

Those past three decades would register as barely a breath in the chronology of time, yet even in the blur of modern life, it signifies the rite of passage between two centuries and two millennia, the old and the new. In those numbered years, wars have been lost and won; governments have changed, walls have fallen, dictatorships brought to an end. The world has moved on, perhaps not always seamlessly, molded, reshaped and reshuffled by both its priorities and its boundaries, defined as much by its secular latter-day inventions as by wisdom learnt. In this new, brave world where everything has become immediate and uniformly accessible, the legacy of what we achieve and how we achieve it is important.

This is the story of Grays of Westminster and the legacy they leave. ■

NIGEL ATHERTON

Nigel Atherton studied photography at Plymouth College of Art & Design and the University of Westminster and worked as a professional photographer for over 10 years before joining *Amateur Photographer* magazine in 1994. He was appointed editor of *What Digital Camera* in 2002, and Group Editor of the *Time Inc* photography portfolio (which includes *Amateur Photographer* and *What Digital Camera*) in 2013. He has also written and edited several books on photography.

"For too many retailers today customer service is a necessary evil, to be performed as quickly and cheaply as possible. Take a ticket and form a queue. Press one for billing, two for technical support, and here's half an hour of Vivaldi's Four Seasons while you wait. Need some buying advice? Read the label on the shelf.

"The days seem long gone where you walk into a shop and are treated like a VIP. But Grays of Westminster is such a place. It reminds me a little of the shop that Mr Benn used to go into in that 1970's children's cartoon series – when you step inside you go back in time to another era.

"Grays of Westminster feels part shop, part museum; its shelves and cabinets overflow with every conceivable item of Nikon equipment past and present. Time seems to slow down within its wood-panelled world. Gray and his team seem to know pretty much everything there is to know about Nikon, and you feel you have all the time you need to ensure that you make the right decision.

"Grays of Westminster is proof that retail doesn't have to be the impersonal, box-shifting exercise that it so often is these days. I congratulate the team on thirty successful years as a Nikon specialist and have every confidence that they will still be around in another thirty."

– Nigel Atherton

CHAPTER 2 IN THE COMPANY OF LEGENDS

In an age that has given rise to mass production and hasty manners, the time-honoured quality of either an exceptional product or exemplary service can be conspicuously uncommon.

At Grays of Westminster, despite the unremitting pace of life, the old ways of doing things are still given importance.

Over the past thirty years they have won numerous awards and distinctions. They are the first camera shop in the world to be granted their own Coat of Arms by Her Majesty's College of Arms. They have been defined and described in multitudinous ways by the photographic community, the media and the 49,000 clients they look after.

No other photographic store in the world is quite like it. It is as though someone has taken a distinguished, elegant gentleman's club of a bygone era, albeit without the ironed newspapers, and fused it seamlessly with a camera store.

Grays of Westminster is in a distinctive period building in a quiet backwater of Westminster, London, just a stone's throw

from Buckingham Palace and the Houses of Parliament. As you enter its tranquil sanctity of deep blue and gold carpeting, chiming clocks, dark-panelled walls and shining brass plate, you could well have slipped unnoticed through a time portal into an earlier era of butlers and fine port. Instead of a crowded counter or the predictable over-labelled window display of the conventional camera retailer of the twenty-first century, here there are leathered desks and regency chairs on which you may sit and ponder while making your acquisitions.

Nikon
Nikon

Nikon
The Choice
EUROPEAN CAMERA OF THE YEAR '89-'90
CAMERA GRAND PRIX '89
The Nikon F4
PROFESSIONAL
Grays of Westminster
Exclusively...
IN THE COMPANY OF LEGENDS
by Gillian Greenwood
MBD11
MBD12
MBD14
MBD15
Nikon FM3A
Nikon FM3AA
F3/T
Nikon
50mm f/1.8G
Gold Edition

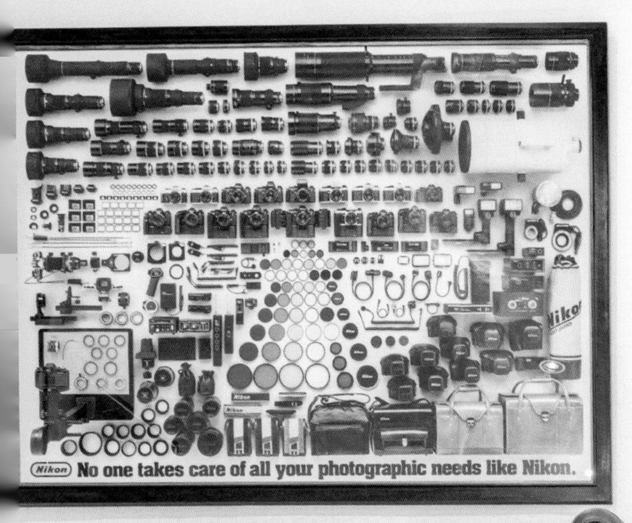
Nikon
No one takes care of all your photographic needs like Nikon.

Nikon

TUESDAY
6
OCTOBER

Nikon OWNER
Eyes of Nikon
NIKON D5500
NIKON D750
NIKON D810
NIKON Df
Nikon
A CELEBRATION
BRIAN LONG
NIKON D3300
NIKON D5300
NIKON D5500
NIKON D3000
NIKON D3300
NIKON D5200
NIKON D7100
NIKON D600

But neither the service you receive nor the equipment displayed is archaic or obsolete. The wooden glass-fronted cabinets are brimming with the latest Nikon DSLRs and Nikkor lenses, and visitors and customers alike can be certain of receiving knowledgeable and unhurried assistance on their purchase, questions answered fully, information given factually and professionally.

Whether it is an instruction booklet, an eyecup for just a few pounds or a lens of over £50,000 in value, the staff of Grays of Westminster are ready to help.

They understand and believe in the equipment they sell and, if you buy your cameras and lenses from them, they will make sure you do as well.

Over the last thirty years, Grays of Westminster have become an international icon of all that is excellent in the way of bespoke service for the Nikon enthusiast and professional alike. It is as much for its service to its customers as for the variety and quality of its Nikon products that Grays of Westminster are renowned.

Despite only dealing with a single brand, Grays of Westminster have consistently won major Good Service Awards, voted for by the public, year after year.

Grays of Westminster have also earned the reputation of having unique access to perhaps the most collectable vintage Nikon cameras on the planet, sourced internationally by their knowledgeable buyers. They have likewise established an unparalleled network of contacts throughout the world, especially Japan, which allows them to track down hard-to-find Nikon products.

Over the years, Grays of Westminster have often assisted collectors from different parts of the globe to amass vintage or contemporary items for their own personal collections.

The Grays of Westminster database includes Nikon users in all seven continents of the world. Because Grays of Westminster is an international and national mail-order service as well as a London retailer, many foreign customers find it quicker to order their equipment from Grays than from the local photographic dealer in their own country. It is not uncommon for foreign visitors to pay a visit to the shop during the morning to order a hard-to-obtain Nikon item, and then fly out of the U.K., their purchase with them later that evening on their return flight.

Whether equipping an expedition to the Galapagos Islands, providing specific difficult-to-obtain lenses to Hollywood, or delivering a lens hood or a Nikkor AF-S 800mm f/5.6E VR FL ED to Malaysia or Buenos Aires, Grays of Westminster will send the item, beautifully, neatly and securely packed to any destination within hours of receiving the order and with as much effortless efficiency as they might deliver a piece of equipment to an address in nearby Knightsbridge or Belgravia.

HEATHER ANGEL
Exploiting Natural Light
OWNER
Nikon
The Choice
The Nikon F4
PROFESSIONAL

No one takes care of all your photographic needs like Nikon.
MONDAY
5
OCTOBER
Nikon
Nikon
Eyes of Nikon
NIKON D5500
NIKON D750
NIKON D810
NIKON Df
Nikon
A CELEBRATION
NIKON D3300
NIKON D5300
NIKON D5500
NIKON D5200
NIKON D7100
NIKON D600
BANDIT SECURITY FOGGING SYSTEM OPERATING HERE
WHEN ACTIVATED A DENSE PLUME OF FOG IS EMITTED AND VISIBILITY WILL BE RAPIDLY IMPAIRED
THE SYSTEM ALSO ACTIONS RAPID POLICE RESPONSE
Grays of Westminster

In fact, providing the item is in stock, or at least in the warehouse, there is almost no item of Nikon equipment that Grays of Westminster is not prepared to send to any client in any part of the globe. There was, for example, the customer that phoned from a remote island off the coast of India; she had dropped an inexpensive but essential Nikon eyepiece into the Indian Ocean the day before and needed a replacement urgently for a vital shoot. Grays replaced this item within forty-eight hours. On another occasion, Grays received a faxed order from the British Antarctic Survey Rothera and rushed the Nikon equipment ordered to Chile to meet the last plane flying into the Base Station before winter set in.

"JUST A QUICK NOTE TO SAY THANKS AGAIN FOR THE TRULY EXTRAORDINARY EFFORTS YOU MADE TO DELIVER MY NEW CAMERA TO ME.... I HAVE NEVER EVER COME ACROSS SUCH AN AMAZINGLY HIGH LEVEL OF CUSTOMER SERVICE, AND WITH SUCH A LACK OF DRAMA, AS IF IT WERE AN EVERYDAY OCCURRENCE!

To some purchasers, the speed and reliability of the Grays of Westminster service has made them into loyal customers for life.

Gray Levett, the founder of Grays of Westminster tells one of the stories:

"We had just sold out of a particular Nikon SLR. A telephone order came in the day that we were due to get a delivery from Nikon U.K.. Sadly, the delivery arrived too late to enable us to send the item which our customer needed urgently the following day. As the long Easter weekend was beginning the day after that, it would have meant that the camera could not be sent until the following Tuesday to arrive Wednesday, making a delay of six days. One of our staff took the decision to catch a train after closing time to the north of England to deliver the camera to the customer. This round journey from start to finish took eight hours. The camera was delivered on the same day it was ordered. Here follows the response from the surprised and delighted customer:

'Just a quick note to say thanks again for the truly extraordinary efforts you made to deliver my new camera to me. I have told many people the full story of what you did. Most people reacted with raised eyebrows! I have never ever come across such an amazingly high level of customer service, and with such a lack of drama, as if it were an everyday occurrence! I could never imagine that a 'set-back' with my order could have been so well handled. I recall saying to you that you had moved heaven and earth."

The same customer wrote to Gray Levett again some years later in 2015 reminding him of that story, and thanking the staff who had helped him with his latest order.

"I will never forget that experience.... It is funny really because these days we live in a world where one can just click a mouse and order something where there is no connection with the vendor. The retail business has changed a lot since then but I am pleased you are still offering a different way. There is something unique about the way you do things." – Jonathan Pledger. ■

Grays of Westminster
25th Anniversary 1985 – 2011
"Grays of Westminster – The High Church of Nikon."
– Professional Photographer magazine
"Grays of Westminster – A true retailing phenomenon."
– BPI – British Photographic Industry News
Look into our body.
Nikon
SB700
NIKKOR
SanDisk

MICHAEL BOND

When Michael Bond was working as a television cameraman for the BBC, he came up with the idea for Paddington and recalls in his own words how this came about:

"I bought a small toy bear on Christmas Eve 1956. I saw it left on a shelf in a London store and felt sorry for it. I took it home as a present for my wife Brenda and named it Paddington as we were living near Paddington Station at the time. I wrote some stories about the bear, more for fun than with the idea of having them published. After ten days I found that I had a book on my hands."

A Bear Called Paddington was published in 1958. Michael Bond went on to write a whole series and by 1965 his books were so successful that he was able to give up working for the BBC. The Paddington books have sold more than thirty-five million copies worldwide and have been translated into over forty languages, including Latin.

In 1997 Michael Bond was awarded an OBE for services to children's literature, followed by a CBE in the Queen's Birthday Honours in 2015. He is still writing and lives in London, not far from Paddington Station where it all began.

"I have yet to read Grays of Westminster ...exclusively Nikon; that is a pleasure still to come, but already I know what to expect. It will be a 'quality' production: the title, with its two key words Grays and Nikon, says it all.

"Such excellence is instantly recognizable; you can see it, feel it, taste it, even smell it. But for all that, it is often hard to pin down as it is to analyze the 'star quality' of, say, the late Rex Harrison or Laurence Olivier.

"The story of Nikon is one of dedication to quality; you only have to hold one of their products in your hand to realize that. Pass through the door of 40 Churton Street, Pimlico, take a look around, and you will find a similar story.

"To parody the well-known song: 'Grays and Nikon go together like a horse and carriage': in culinary terms, the French would say it is 'un bon marriage', and in a world where all too often standards seem to be falling around us, these are things to cherish!"

– Michael Bond (creator of Paddington Bear)

CHAPTER 3
A DAY IN THE LIFE

It might seem to the customer or client that Grays of Westminster have achieved their success with an inexplicable form of effortlessness. But the mystical image of an unhurried pace belies the sheer volume of the business that comes their way and the hard work that goes on behind the scenes.

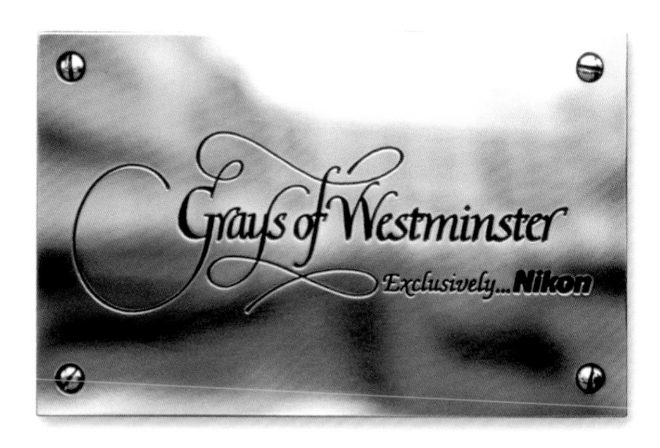

The day at Grays of Westminster starts early. At six o'clock of a summer morning, Billy 'the Brass' White can be seen in the early morning light, polishing the brass, cleaning the windows to herald in another day. Long before the shop opens, the staff arrive to answer their emailed queries or orders and complete the volume of their international email correspondence before the working day begins.

At ten o'clock, the doors are unlocked with the precision of timing reminiscent of the start of a journey of the celebrated Japanese Bullet Train.

As if by magic, the phones leap to life even as the first customers file in. They may decide to sit on the comfortable leathered chairs while waiting to be served or instead to view one of the equipment displays. Each and every customer is treated to a cheerful welcome and is attended to promptly.

The first query is whether or not Grays can get a now-discontinued and ultra-rare UV-Nikkor lens to be sent to a research laboratory in the U.S.A. before the weekend.

The next customer tells a member of staff that she no longer has her much loved Nikon F3/T (Titanium) camera and regrets having sold it. She is taken to the vintage section in the Nippon Kogaku Room on the lower ground floor and she is delighted to find a mint, boxed example in one of the glass cabinets.

“

THE FIRST QUERY IS WHETHER OR NOT GRAYS CAN GET A NOW-DISCONTINUED AND ULTRA-RARE UV-NIKKOR LENS TO BE SENT TO A RESEARCH LABORATORY IN THE U.S.A. BEFORE THE WEEKEND.

”

Elsewhere a member of staff is discussing with a young man and his wife some discouraging photographs taken on their holiday. The problem is isolated and a solution to the problem is found. Another customer has been informed by her local camera shop that Nikon only make one colour and size of camera strap: black and narrow. She leaves the shop a few moments later with a wide maroon Nikon strap, her face a mixture of mortification and triumph.

Periodically throughout the day, enormous cartons of Nikon equipment arrive, forming vast, majestic stacks in the lobby. Throughout the day too, drivers collect and deliver equipment for service and repair to and from the workshops. High-profile clients who wish to avoid the public gaze are discreetly ushered upstairs to the founder's office. Any questions or comments from the public as to the status of the individual, photographic or otherwise, are treated with a firm 'we could not possibly comment'.

The shipping supervisor and her team make their way into the cavernous non-public area in the lower floor and using the finest materials available start to pack with immense care all the orders that have been issued so far for that day. They do not consider their day has finished until the shelves in the packing department are completely empty.

Meanwhile the flow of customers is uninterrupted, each one leaving with the distinctive navy-blue carrier bag inscribed with the gold copperplate lettering of Grays of Westminster…exclusively Nikon. As the day continues, representatives from UPS, DHL and FedEx jockey for access to the parcels awaiting for collection. Their vans appear outside of the shop and disappear discreetly, whisking away their cargo of DSLR cameras, lenses and flashguns to far-away places, such as Brunei, South Georgia and Swaziland. The telephone rings continuously as mail orders are taken; the shop is full to brimming but each customer is served and questions answered without stint of time or patience.

All too quickly the day ends as the team from Royal Mail arrive to supervise their load quickly and efficiently, providing their regular collection and overnight delivery service for the U.K. outgoing packages. Even now, as the clock strikes five, their exit is blocked by a member of staff trying to get a customer's late order into the post so that it will arrive the next day for an important photographic deadline. The last customer lingers, his bags full of Nikon bodies, Nikkor lenses, accessories and books, hesitant to leave, as if unwilling to return to the abrupt, commercial machinations of the real world.

Finally, the door is locked and the silver shutters are fastened shut; as the vintage items are carefully returned to the glass fronted cabinets, the cleaning team arrives to take over.

Another day ends at Grays of Westminster. ■

GARRY COWARD-WILLIAMS

Garry Coward-Williams left school at 15 to become a roadie for The Stranglers before deciding on a proper career in photography. He worked as an advertising photographer in London's West End for ten years and then moved into magazine publishing. In 1998 he became editor of *Amateur Photographer*, the world's oldest photographic journal, which he edited for ten years before being appointed head of research and development of Time Inc's specialist magazines.

"Grays of Westminster is probably the finest Nikon emporium in the world'. Forgive my conceptual theft, or plagiarism of an old advertisement for a Scandinavian lager, but I could not resist.

"I use the term 'emporium' because it expresses what Grays of Westminster actually is far more accurately than a mere 'camera shop' or 'photographic retailer' — those latter descriptions appear almost insulting in comparison.

"For me an emporium conjures up something both romantically and practically Victorian. Stepping into Grays is like stepping back to a time when the highest quality service was a requirement, not a rare surprise. When etiquette wasn't just a tricky word to spell, it was at the cornerstone of all customer interaction, as it demonstrated due respect and appreciation to clients.

"Grays of Westminster is many things to me:

"A club: the décor and general ambience of its premises call to mind an exclusive London club and yet it is open to all. And of course, Grays is a club…it is a Nikon owners' club. I have met many members of this august society and they are all as charming as they are enthusiastic and talented.

"A treasure trove of all things Nikon: a place where beautiful wooden cabinets contain highly rare and much-sought-after Nikon products from the pre-digital age, as well as the most up-to-date, state-of-the-art Nikon technology.

"It is the home of friends: for I have always been made so welcome and so very special, as though I were a duke, rather than a commoner; I have come to know the never-changing staff (the sign of a true emporium) and always look forward to seeing them again.

"A fountain of knowledge and advice: Grays of Westminster is unrivalled in its Nikon lore, and I always gravitate to genuine expertise.

"Finally there is Gray Levett himself: in my allegory I see him as the inspired protégée of H.G. Wells, who took us back in his own photographic time machine to show us all what a genuine Nikon emporium could be… and then he made it all come true."

– Garry Coward-Williams

CHAPTER 4
WRITING WITH LIGHT

1985 was a year of legends, of extraordinary people and extraordinary accomplishments.

In July of that year, the historic Live Aid Concert, in response to Sir Bob Geldof's astoundingly successful Band Aid single *Do They Know It's Christmas?* released in late 1984, took place simultaneously in London and Philadelphia and was immortalised on television all over the planet. Almost a hundred musicians played throughout the concert, many of them towering performers such as U2, Sting, Ozzy Osbourne and Black Sabbath, Phil Collins, David Bowie, Brian Ferry, Dire Straits, Mick Jagger, Elton John, Paul McCartney, Madonna and Eric Clapton. Live Aid raised over $100,000,000 for victims of the famine in Ethiopia.

In March of the same year, Mikhail Gorbachev had become the General Secretary of the Communist Party, thereby bringing his auspicious career as President of the Soviet Union closer to attainment.

In September, the wreckage of R.M.S. Titanic was finally found by Dr Robert D. Ballard Ph.D. and momentously filmed by a robotic camera.

Julia Margaret Cameron

When Gray Levett founded Grays of Westminster in November of the same year, photography had achieved its own legendary status in the world of photo-journalism, in fashion, in portraiture, in wildlife and as a pure art-form.

The timeline of great photography had from the beginning interwoven an uninterrupted pattern with correlative development in camera and equipment design. From the eminent romantic portrait photographers of the nineteenth century, such as Julia Margaret Cameron, who famously photographed the poet Tennyson, to the avant-garde surrealist Man Ray, from the sweeping landscapes of

Ansel Adams to the sharply noted 'decisive moment' of Henri Cartier-Bresson, or the grim war images of Margaret Bourke-White and Robert Capa, photography had moved forward, embracing social, political and technological changes.

Man's desire to capture evanescent images is perhaps an unspoken fundamental need, a simple requirement to make his life less fragile, less transient, enabling him to turn his own aspirations away from the sense of mortality and towards the goal of eternity. Whether the accomplished drawings of prehistoric bison and lions etched some 31,000 years ago on the walls of the Chauvet-Pont-d'Arc cave, the flawless illuminations executed by monks in the Book of Kells, or contemporary abstractions profoundly fixed on photographic paper, Man is fascinated by images, both his own and others'.

French photographer Louis Daguerre

Likewise, his intrigue with the mystical forces and the primal alchemy of light and dark had been with him long before the first Camera Obscura[1] had formed flickering images in darkened rooms. The 'Darkroom' itself had been in existence for at least four hundred years prior to its own final partnership with twentieth century photography. Leonardo da Vinci had made an accomplished drawing of a Camera Obscura as far back as 1519.

Many of the scientific processes that combine to make photography possible had been known about and understood for some time, but it was only with the exact combination of optics and chemistry that a 'picture' could be produced.

It was Nicéphore Niepce who produced the first successful picture in 1826, using material that hardened on exposure to light. On his death, his partner Louis Daguerre continued to experiment, creating single images, but discovered how to make the images permanent. In the meantime, William Henry Fox Talbot had produced the earliest paper negative in August 1834 and today's photography is based on the Fox Talbot principle: the creation of an unlimited number of prints, rather than the 'one-off' image produced by Niepce and Daguerre.

Sir John Herschel is attributed to having first used the term 'photography' in 1839, the year the photographic process became public. The word is derived from the Greek words for light and writing, and with some license could be described poetically as 'writing with light'.

Like Galileo and many others before and after him, new movements and ideas, whether humanist or scientific, are often harshly attacked before being absorbed into the mainstream. A contemporary newspaper report in the *Leipzig City Advertiser* in 1839 on these early 'cameras', stated: "*God created man in His own image, and no man-made machine may fix the image of God. Is it possible that God should have abandoned His eternal principles, and allowed a Frenchman [Daguerre]… to give to the world an invention of the Devil?*"

1921 Take a "Kodak" with you.
The girl in the striped dress by Fred Pegram.

The Calypso/ Nikkor II underwater camera circa 1968

But by the end of the nineteenth century, helped by the development of first the collodion[2] process in 1851 by Frederick Scott Archer, then the use of gelatin, discovered by Dr Richard Maddox in 1871 as a basis for the photographic plate instead of glass, a new era in photography had begun.

The introduction of flexible film in 1884 by George Eastman and four years later his box camera incorporating roll film, with the slogan 'You press the button, we do the rest', meant that photography could now reach a much greater number of people.

Up to the time of George Eastman, photography, though already popular, was still considered too complicated for ordinary users, and Eastman is remembered quite rightly for having made photography accessible to everyone.

By the end of the nineteenth century, processes had been developed which led to wider photographic application and photography was regularly used to record people and places.

In 1900 the Kodak Brownie box roll-film cameras were introduced. The first Kodak cameras had appeared first of all with a twenty-foot roll of paper.

Colour film was not far behind, and in 1907 the first commercial colour film, the Autochrome plates, was manufactured by the Lumiere brothers in France, although it was not until the much later date of 1936 that the development of Kodachrome, the first multi-layered colour film occurred.

In 1917 Nippon Kogaku K.K., which eventually become Nikon, was established in Tokyo.

Initial development and research by Oscar Barnack, while under the employ of the German microscope manufacturer Leitz, was later modified in 1924 to develop the first high-quality 35mm camera, with the Rolleiflex twin-lens reflex producing a 6 x 6cm image on roll film in 1928.

Pioneering 35mm single-lens reflex (SLR) cameras were later used in World War II. In 1948, Hasselblad in Sweden offered its first medium-format SLR for commercial sale, and in 1949, the East German Zeiss developed the Contax S, the first SLR with an unreversed image in a pentaprism viewfinder.

“THE INTRODUCTION OF FLEXIBLE FILM IN 1884 BY GEORGE EASTMAN AND FOUR YEARS LATER HIS BOX CAMERA INCORPORATING ROLL FILM, WITH THE SLOGAN 'YOU PRESS THE BUTTON, WE DO THE REST', MEANT THAT PHOTOGRAPHY COULD NOW REACH A MUCH GREATER NUMBER OF PEOPLE.

With the introduction of the innovative Nikon F in 1959 and the very first purpose-built underwater camera, the Nikonos in 1963, the basis for the modern camera and for Nikon's own advent into world-league photographic equipment was well under way. ■

DAMIEN DEMOLDER

Damien is a photographer, journalist and photographic equipment expert, speaker, judge and educator. He has worked in the photographic publishing industry for 18 years, including 15 years at the world's only weekly photo magazine, *Amateur Photographer*, where he was editor. Today his technical tests and photography reviews appear in *Amateur Photographer, Digital Photography Review* and the *British Journal of Photography*.

He uses a wide range of equipment, from wooden plate cameras to the latest DSLRs, and is a great fan of all products that make good photography more accessible to more people.

Although he specialises in street photography, he also shoots portraits, landscapes, architecture, natural macro and occasionally even wildlife and weddings.
https://damiendemolder.com

"I think I would find it immensely embarrassing to go camera shopping with an engineer or designer from the Nikon factory. The detail, care and attention that goes into even the lowliest D series DSLR – from the feel of the grip to the new slight modification to the flash mode, the new sync speed, the refined post-capture editing or the adjusted processing that provides a cleaner print-ready JPEG file – is so often lost, missed and neglected by the salesman who sees only another box to shift.

"It is heart-breaking too that those considering a DSLR for the first time, who most need, and very reasonably expect, the guidance of someone with their interests in mind can often meet ignorance, dishonesty and lack of duty. Unengaged, poorly paid and under-trained staff, who are constantly on the move, are the symptoms of an industry that has forgotten its focus and purpose.

"It's sad that's the experience for the majority of the population when they come to buy a camera, but thankfully not all photographic outlets are the same. If there was needed an example of how things could be done, Grays of Westminster would be the obvious choice. The customer may not always know what it is that he wants or needs, but he will leave the store comfortable in the knowledge that he now has the right camera, lens or accessory – AND is in possession of the right footing to get the best from it. He will have been served by someone who listened to his problems and requirements, and who solved them with questioning and attention to detail.

"Grays isn't a shrine to Nikon, it is a shrine to customer service. It is a working exhibition of Nikon products throughout the ages that visitors are welcome to pick up, try out, have explained, and ultimately take home for their own continued enjoyment. It is a meeting of minds, a club in which all are welcome and an institution. Above all though, it is a truly extraordinary shop: a shop that has respect – for its customers, for the goods on sale, for the people that made them, for photography, for the past, the present and for the future – at the very core of its being."

– Damien Demolder

CHAPTER 5
THE ROAD TO DISCOVERY

There is a history in all men's lives[3].

Gray Levett, the distinguished founder of Grays of Westminster, was born a few years after the end of the Second World War into a sombre Britain of ration books and grim winters. This was a world still governed by the economic order of form and edifice: an unbending class structure, a frequently dreary workplace and a workforce clothed in the unvarying uniformity of grey overalls at the worst, grey suits and bowler-hats at the best. For many, it was an unfulfilled, pedestrian existence with just a vague hope of promotion or happiness; a cheap bottle of sherry, a limp handshake or a malevolent watch was often the only reward at the end of lifelong service.

Yet within two decades life had changed abruptly. With the emergence of the culture of youth and the brightly fashioned new world of the nineteen-sixties and 'seventies, the impetus of change swept forward in glaring op-art technicolor with a recklessness and a force that was the equivalent to ramming two tectonic plates together; it seemed that the monochromatic world of nineteen-fifties' Britain might disappear forever.

Gray was part of the young generation of that time who were confronted by the collision of conflicting values and ideologies in disarray.

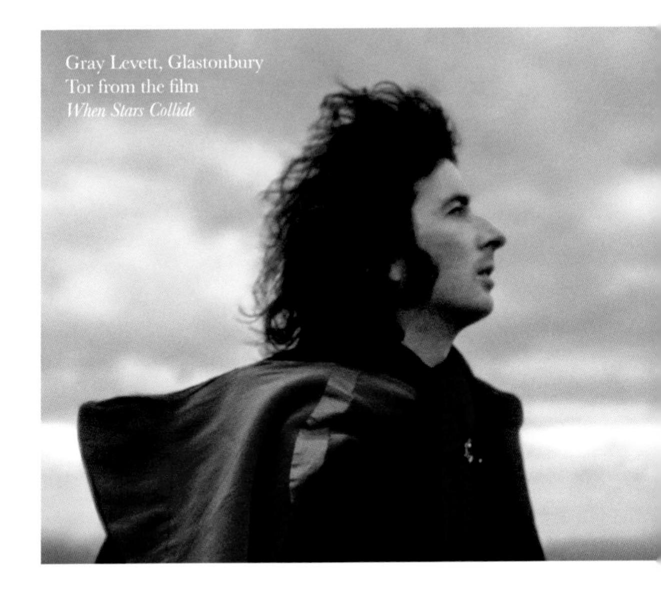
Gray Levett, Glastonbury Tor from the film *When Stars Collide*

The catalyst for the upheaval was the catastrophe of the Vietnam War and the cult of 'flower-power' followed by the idealistic and rebellious student movement, creating altogether a dynamic energy that caused a revolution in thought, in fashion, and in music. 1968 was a pivotal year that accelerated the new mood of the youth counterculture. Martin Luther King was tragically murdered in Memphis on April

4th. The student revolution occurred in May 1968 in France, with virtual open warfare in the streets of Paris. Protests in the U.K. were heralded by the students of the London School of Economics in London, marching to the cries of *'London, Paris, Rome, Berlin, we shall fight, and we will win'*. Further riots took place in Turin, Madrid, New York, Bonn, Frankfurt, Warsaw and Berlin, as tens of thousands of students across the world started to participate in mutual struggles in direct confrontation to the existing state of affairs.

Che Guevara T-shirts, well-thumbed copies of *Das Kapital,* searing rock music, protest songs: the tone and the mood of the youth counterculture was intoxicating. The broadly-sourced virtuosity of the Beatles in *Revolution #1*, the Rolling Stones in *Street Fighting Man,* Jimi Hendrix's guitar pyrotechnics permeated all elements of society and exerted a pervasive influence on fashion, social and sexual mores. In the summer of 1969, a crowd of 400,000 descended on Woodstock, New York, in a communal celebration of youthful solidarity and electrified rock. A new world order seemed at hand.

Gray's summer holidays spent on Bournemouth Beach

Gray had moved with his family to Bournemouth on the South Coast of England at the age of seven. The son of an RAF officer wounded during the Second World War, Gray disliked the stringently formulated disciplines of school and rebelled against its rigours with a passion. In his teenage years, he worked for a while at a 'Carnaby Street' styled clothes boutique, called Lord Peter. The timing was coincident with the contemporaneous young British fashion scene of the period, which included such luminaries such as Ossie Clark, Mary Quant, Zandra Rhodes and Barbara Hulanicki of Biba, and was a pageant of vivid colours, op-art, mini-skirts, shimmering chiffons, velvets, kaftans, beads and body paint. While Gray was working at the boutique, he and his colleagues would often be asked to pose for pictures, but he soon found that he was more interested in the picture-taking process than being on the other side of the camera. Thus he ventured into photography more by chance than by intent.

It was against this backdrop of emotive social change that Gray found himself with choices and decisions to make with regard to his own future. It was Michelangelo Antonioni's provocative masterpiece, *Blow-up*, released in 1966, nominated for two Academy Awards and starring David Hemmings using a Nikon F, that was the catalyst. The film included a sequence of The Yardbirds, featuring Jimmy Page and Jeff Beck, and precipitated Gray's growing interest not only in rock music, but photography in general and Nikon in particular. ■

Gray Levett's Nikon F

MICHAEL DOVEN

Michael Doven has been making striking images since 1977. By the age of 25, Michael had already travelled extensively and logged trips to over 50 countries across the globe.

In 1991 Michael embarked on a twenty-year journey in feature film production in Hollywood where he was blessed, being able to watch, study and learn from amongst the greatest directors of photography in the world, while serving as Associate-Producer on many films.

Michael's unique perspective and composition lend a timeless spirituality and vividness to his images. Michael Doven's Fine Art Photography is represented by Christie's International Auctions Worldwide. His editorial and portrait work graces worldwide covers as well and is seen by hundreds of millions.

To view more of his works visit:
www.dovengallery.com and
www.michaeldoven.com

G

"Grays of Westminster in London continues to lead the U.K. and Europe in NIKON sales, service, seminars, workshops, magazines and has done so now for over 30 years.

"The exceptional service provided and personal attention to each customer and his unique needs has earned respect from professionals and royalty alike.

"The true professional cares about his gear and the details involved in the purchase, sale or service and the reputation of those he works with, as it is a reflection on himself. In this regard, Grays of Westminster has no peer. In other words, Grays is the ONLY place to go to get the most professional gear, service or training.

"Gray Levett and his extremely able and accomplished staff and associates understand the responsibility they have taken on and wear the honor easily. Frankly, they make NIKON look very good and showcase the entire Nikon line past, present and future like nowhere else in the world.

"If I were NIKON, I would send you multiple awards. Oh wait, they already have done so, numerous times!

"Okay, then I will send you mine:

"I hereby commend Grays of Westminster for 30 years of exceptional service and sales, setting the example for others to follow.

"Thank you for all that you do for us in the Nikon Professional community!"

– Michael Doven
NPS (Nikon Professional Services) member

CHAPTER 6
THE FORMATION OF NIKON

Mount Fuji, Japan's highest mountain, rises above the clouds with the sculptured symmetry of a lotus flower. Legend has it that in the ancient days the Goddess of Fuji hovered in a luminous cloud above the crater, tended by invisible servants who were prepared to throw down any pilgrims who were not pure of heart.

The mountain's venerated presence is still felt throughout Japan, and it is perhaps no accident that it was the Fuji Building in Tokyo that housed the Headquarters of the Nikon Corporation for many years.

From 1917 until the present day, the Nikon brand has been associated with purity of conception and intelligence of design, a formula that has become legendary.

All legends have to start somewhere, and Nikon's began on 20th July 1917 when Nippon Kogaku (Kogyo Kaisha) was formed by the merger of three of Japan's leading optical manufacturers. Nippon Kogaku means Japan Optical Company. The name Nikon apparently comes from the first letters of NIppon KOgaku to which the letter 'N' was added.

Their beginnings mirror that of Leitz and Zeiss who also started life as optical manufacturers. Nikon produced high-quality optical products, such as microscopes, telescopes and surveying instruments.

The logo used on Nippon Kogaku's very early letterheads.

The symbol used on the company flag, designed in 1930.

The official Nippon Kogaku logo, circa 1930.

The logo adopted just after the birth of the Nikon camera.

NIPPON KOGAKU K. K.
日 本 光 学 工 業 株 式 会 社

LEFT: The English and Japanese typeface styles used from May 1954.

The revised company logo, widely adopted from 1962.

An alternative logo to the 1962 version, used from July 1967.

NIKON CORPORATION
株式会社 ニコン
Nikon

LEFT: The English and Japanese typeface styles registered in 1987 but used from April 1988, plus the new company logo introduced at the same time.

Logos courtesy of Brian Long from his book Nikon A Celebration, The Crowood Press 2011

By 1932 they were producing photographic lenses and it was then that the name 'Nikkor' was first used to identify their lenses. This name derived from 'Nikko', which was used on their early microscopes. The term 'nikko' also means 'resplendent light' or 'the sun', which gives an almost metaphysical imagery to the brand. The word Nikkor first appeared on a 10.5cm f/4.5 lens mounted on the Lily Hand camera. It is a little-known fact that until 1947, Nikon produced all of Canon's lenses for their Hansa Canon cameras. Nikon continued in this fashion, producing lenses but had yet to manufacture a camera of their own.

The first camera put into commercial production was the Nikon Model One in March 1948. This first-ever Nikon 35mm camera featured a focal plane shutter with rangefinder focusing and a format size of 24 x 32mm. It was fitted with the 5cm f/2 Nikkor lens, the first Nikkor lens to have a Nikon bayonet mount.

Masahiko Fuketa original designer of the Nikon One

But the decision to use a 24 x 32mm format was a mistake as it made their camera incompatible with automated colour slide cutting machines in the U.S.A.. Because of this, only very few Nikon Model Ones made their way to the U.S.A. although some were sold to Occupation troops via the 'PX' shops. It was replaced in 1950 by the Nikon M (the M standing for mutatio, Latin for change or alteration). The M used a 24 x 34mm format, but it was still smaller than the 24 x 36mm employed by Leica. Nippon Kogaku replaced the Nikon M in January 1951 with the Nikon S camera. The Nikon S retained all the features of the M including the film format. It also offered flash synchronization. The S continued in production for three years.

In the spring of 1950, David Douglas Duncan, a *LIFE* magazine photographer, visited Japan to take pictures of traditional Japanese fine arts. While he was there, Duncan made a fortuitous discovery when his assistant, a young Japanese photographer, Mr. Jun Miki, took his photograph. Duncan was so impressed by the results he asked to be taken to the manufacturer Nippon Kogaku KK (Nikon) to examine the Nikkor lenses and compare them with his favourite Leicas. He started testing a 35mm f/3.5 and one camera body, spending about a week doing the tests.

David Douglas Duncan

As a result of this, Duncan bought a complete set of Nikkor lenses. Two days later on Sunday, June 25th, war broke out in Korea. He was sent with General MacArthur to fly

Hansa Canon

Nippon Kogaku factory 1952

him the U.S. Camera Prize in 1950. Midan's Nikkor lens stood him in equally good stead, for he too won the same prize for his outstanding pictures. On December 10th 1950 the *New York Times* featured a full article on the emergence of Nikon's use in the ranks of professional photojournalists.

The subsequent article by Jacob Deschin had much to say in praise of Nikon: *"The first post-war Japanese camera to attract serious attention in America has created a sensation among magazine and press photographers following the report by LIFE photographers in Korea that a Japanese 35mm camera and its lenses had proved superior to the German cameras they had been using. .... The lenses, which include a full range of focal lengths, are the Nikkor, to which American experts give a higher accuracy rating than the lenses available from the German miniatures."*

down to Fukuoka. *LIFE* magazine cabled Duncan after receiving his first photographs in New York, asking, *"Why are you using a plate camera?"* The photographs were so sharp that within a matter of weeks every 'staff man' passing through Tokyo bought himself a set of Nikkor lenses.

When Karl Midans and Hank Walker, two photojournalists additionally covering the Korean War, arrived in Tokyo, they also purchased Nikkors. (Walker took the Nikon S body as well.) Carrying their new equipment, the two men flew to the Korean peninsula. It was a cold winter that year, with temperatures around −30°C. The photojournalists had a hard time; cameras were freezing and ceasing to function. But not Hank Walker's new Nikon S. Not only did it work perfectly even in these harsh conditions, it also produced the magnificent photographs that won

Zeiss were quick with their response to this extraordinary accolade given to a Japanese camera and lens manufacturer.

"The lenses tested up against the Nikkors were not genuine Zeiss lenses!" retorted Doctor Karl Bauer President of Carl Zeiss in the U.S.A. furiously. The debate continued. Michael James in a special report from Tokyo for the *New York Times* on the 9th February 1951 wrote: *"The Japanese are making a bid to take over a large portion of the international precision market. .... [The] success of one company, Nippon Kogaku*

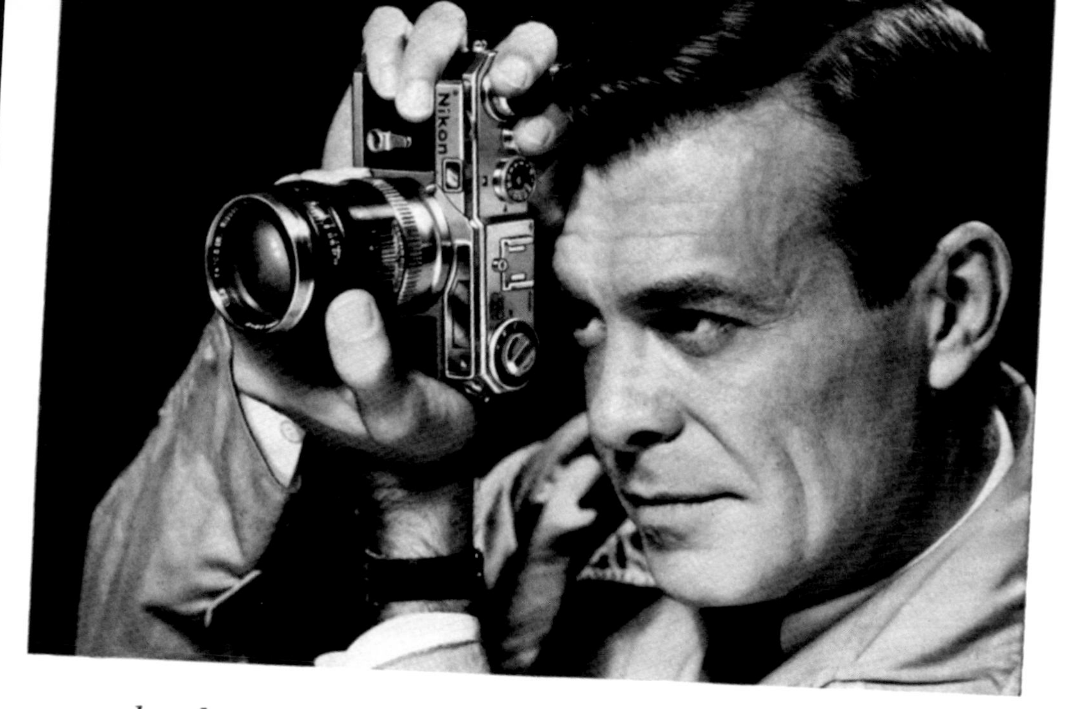

why the man who prefers a rangefinder prefers the

NIKON SP

Ask the man who uses a Nikon SP the reasons for his preference, and invariably he will mention these four:

1 – THE UNIVERSAL VIEWFINDER SYSTEM because it has built-in finders for six focal length lenses – 28, 35, 50, 85, 105 and 135mm – four with automatic parallax compensation. And, as a previewer, it helps him select the right lens faster and easier. *Only the Nikon SP offers you a 6-lens Universal Viewfinder System.*

2 – THE NIKKOR LENSES because of their outstanding resolution and color rendition, even at maximum apertures. For as important as lens interchangeability is to a '35', equally important is the quality of the lenses and the consistency of that quality in all the focal lengths.

Any lens maker who can produce an outstanding lens or two or three, has reason to be proud. *But, only Nikon offers you 20 outstanding lenses – 20 incomparable Nikkor lenses – ranging from 21mm ultra wide angle to 1000mm super telephoto.*

3 – THE ELECTRIC MOTOR DRIVE because this remarkable compact accessory brings to the already versatile Nikon SP an even greater effectiveness – *automatic fire power.* Battery operated, it can be used anywhere – to shoot single exposures, bursts of 2, 3 or more – right through an entire 36-exposure roll – at a rate of up to 3 per second. A fleeting expression, a quick gesture, a dramatic action sequence – you can't miss! *Only Nikon offers you an Electric Motor Drive.*

4 – ITS 'ADVANCE-FOCUS-SHOOT' HANDLING EASE because as important as quality, features and versatility are to a '35', equally important is the speed and ease with which they can be brought into play. The effortless, 3-finger handling of the Nikon SP is one of the secrets of its smooth responsiveness, its speed in action, its uncanny ability to meet the challenge of any situation and emerge with great pictures. *Only Nikon offers you 'Advance-Focus-Shoot' handling ease.*

These are the four essential reasons he will give you for preferring the Nikon SP – if you ask him. Fundamentally, he is interested in results. He expects the finest, and he has every right to, for the instrument he is using is the finest rangefinder-coupled '35' money can buy.

Nikon SP with 50mm Nikkor f/2 lens, $329.50; with f/1.4 $375 at your Nikon Dealer. For complete details write for illustrated brochure to Dept. PP-11.

Nikon Inc., 111 Fifth Avenue, N. Y. 3
In Canada: Anglophoto, Ltd.
880 Champagneur, Montreal, P. Q.

November, 1959

29

(Japan Optical), indicates that the Japanese are already giving stiff competition to the Germans, who once had a virtual monopoly on the field".

The first account in a photographic magazine came in Bruce Downes' article in *Popular Photography* of February 1951 and was entitled *Assignment Korea*, the inside story of David Douglas Duncan and his dramatic coverage of the Korean War. It occupied a full ten pages. This was because Duncan's photographs were of such superb quality and were taken on the hitherto unknown Nikon and Nikkor equipment, not the almost universally used German equivalents. This further favourable publicity was an ideal catalyst for Nikon's growth, which was shortly to become very rapid. Indeed, as *A History of Japanese Cameras* comments, *"(It) came together as an explosive combination that set in train the sudden, dramatic development of the Japanese photographic industry."*

Nikon SP black finish with 5cm f/1.1 Nikkor-N plus S36 motor drive

> "THE ZENITH OF NIKON'S ACHIEVEMENT IN THE NIKON RANGEFINDER SYSTEM WAS THE NIKON SP. IT WAS INTRODUCED IN SEPTEMBER 1957."

An entire book of these unique and special photographs was published in June of that year. The book was entitled *This is War* by David Douglas Duncan.

In order to compete in the world market, Nikon had to make a number of changes to compete with the German cameras, which were again emerging as top brands. These changes manifested themselves in the shape of the Nikon S2 in December 1954.

The S2 was the first Japanese camera to incorporate a film advance lever and a film rewind crank instead of knobs. It also included a life-size viewfinder, which projected a bright line frame to cover the standard 50mm lens. It was the first rangefinder camera offering a 1000 sec. shutter speed and the first Nikon camera offering full-frame 35mm 24x36mm format. The S2 was a much easier and quicker camera to operate. It became very popular amongst photojournalists. In fact the three largest photographic magazines in the U.S.A., *Modern Photography, U.S. Camera* and *Photography*, stated that many photojournalists had taken to using the Nikon S2 camera.

Due to the success of the S2 model, Nippon Kogaku found themselves competing with the other three major 35mm camera manufacturers, Canon, Leica and Zeiss. Nikon had recognised that, with the introduction of the Leica M3 in 1954, they needed to pull out all the stops to improve on the S2. This they did magnificently with the Nikon SP.

It was introduced in September 1957 and became the zenith of Nikon's achievement in the Nikon rangefinder system.

The P stood for Professional and with this model Nikon had created their finest and most innovative rangefinder camera. The SP was unique and was a complete change from all the models that had gone before. The viewfinder of the SP was the most comprehensive ever made; covering nearly half the width of the camera, it gave the SP its distinctive appearance. The viewfinder had projected parallax corrected frame lines for 50, 85, 105 and 135mm lenses, each one being introduced by a lens field selector dial. To the left of the viewfinder there were field frames for 28mm and 35mm lenses that were fixed in position. The SP offered shutter speed settings of 1 to 1/1000 sec., 'B' and 'T' on a rotating shutter speed dial. The SP was the first camera to have a self-timer, an automatic resetting frame counter and a motor drive lug to allow the camera to be motorized.

The SP created a sensation when it was released and helped forge Nikon's dominance in the field of motorized photography that it continues to enjoy today. The S36 motor drive was electrically powered and offered a fixed speed of 3fps (frames per second).

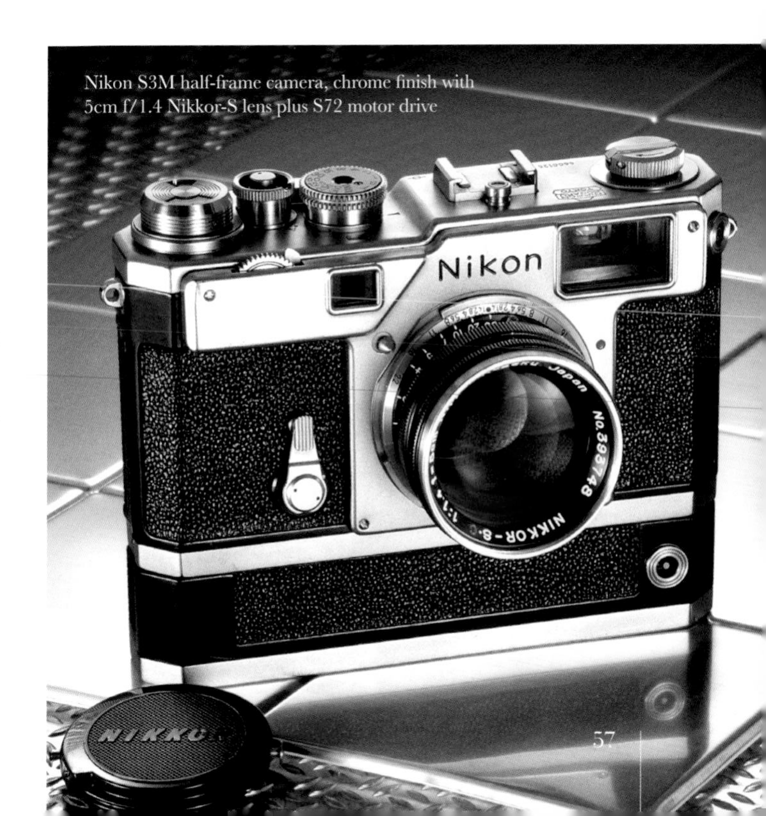

Nikon S3M half-frame camera, chrome finish with 5cm f/1.4 Nikkor-S lens plus S72 motor drive

It should be remembered that apart from the long-discontinued electric motor drive on the rare Leica 250 from World War II, only spring-wound motors such as the Leica Mooly and the Bell & Howell Foton were available. The SP was the only camera that had been designed from the ground up to use a motor drive. The SP was a truly unique camera and fully deserves its high placing amongst the most collectable of all Nikon rangefinder cameras.

In March 1958, following on the heels of the SP, Nikon released the S3. The S3 was designed for those wanting to enter the Nikon system without paying as much as the cost of the SP. The S3 also made an ideal second body for those who already owned an SP. Instead of using projected, parallax-corrected frame lines for lenses, it used a standard viewfinder with etched lines. This was followed by the Nikon S4, which was a simplified version of the S3. It was announced in March 1959 and immediately ran into problems. The U.S. distributor Joseph Ehrenreich refused to bring it into the U.S.A.. He was awaiting the release of the Nikon F single lens reflex and already had the SP and S3. From his point of view, the S4 would only detract from sales of the S3. It is for this reason that the S4 was sold only to the home market.

In April 1960 the last rangefinder camera made by Nikon was released: the Nikon S3M. It was unique in being the first half-frame Nikon camera. What made the S3M different was that the 'M' stood for motorized. Because of its 17 x 24mm half-frame format, it allowed 72mm frames from a 36-exposure film and was supplied with a Nikon S72 motor drive, which gave framing rates of up to twelve frames per second. What makes this model even more unique is that it is also the rarest as only one hundred and ninety-five were ever manufactured.

There are probably few that would argue that the Nikon F, designed to meet the demands of the hard-working professional photographer, was very possibly the most successful and well-known 35mm single lens reflex camera of the 1960s, and the first high-quality SLR to challenge the 35mm rangefinder systems which were used at the time by photojournalists throughout the world. It is still considered to be one of the most famous cameras produced by Nikon.

There are some products that get everything right for the time – such as a Zippo lighter, a Maglite or a Jaguar XK150. So it was with the Nikon F single lens reflex camera. Introduced to the world in June 1959, Nikon got the design of the camera and the system so right that they sold a million of them between 1959 and 1974. It was the first Japanese SLR to have interchangeable focusing screens, depth-of-field preview, mirror lock-up, one hundred percent exact field coverage in the viewfinder, provision for a motor drive and dual-coupled metering. It was a 35mm SLR of outstanding quality, precision, versatility and durability and these components became the standard features expected for any self-respecting 35mm SLR, maintained through subsequent 35mm flagship models up to and including the Nikon F6.

Like the world around it in the nineteen-sixties and nineteen-seventies, as images of life shattered and re-formed, paradoxically the nature of photography too began to change. Nikon instinctively grasped the mood, and with insight and skill produced some of the best cameras and lenses ever manufactured. ■

An early Nikon F camera with 5cm f/2 Nikkor-S lens

> LIKE THE WORLD AROUND IT IN THE NINETEEN-SIXTIES AND NINETEEN-SEVENTIES, AS IMAGES OF LIFE SHATTERED AND RE-FORMED, PARADOXICALLY THE NATURE OF PHOTOGRAPHY TOO BEGAN TO CHANGE. NIKON INSTINCTIVELY GRASPED THE MOOD, AND WITH INSIGHT AND SKILL PRODUCED SOME OF THE BEST CAMERAS AND LENSES EVER MANUFACTURED.

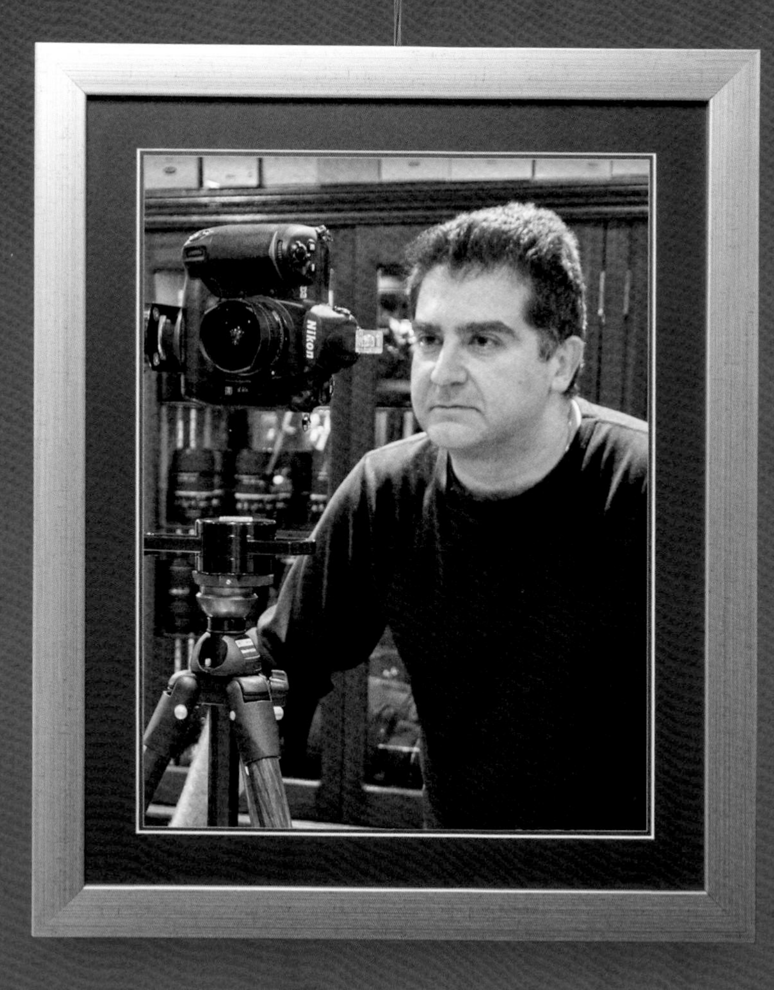

MICHAEL ELEFTHERIADES

Michael Eleftheriades is an architect and highly respected photographer who fuses his particular passion for architecture, virtual reality, computer graphics and photography in the creation of large-scale panoramic imagery. He has exhibited his photographs at three exhibitions in London and lectured on panoramic creation to wide acclaim in the U.K., Europe and the United States. When not photographing, Michael directs the efforts of Media Synthesis, a media development and consultancy company established in 1993, and is responsible for virtual reality tours and interactive exhibits at many of the U.K.'s leading museums, including the Maritime and Natural History Museums.

Michael created the virtual tour for Grays of Westminster and has been the *Nikon Owner* London Group coordinator since 2007.

"Grays of Westminster is not a 'shop' in the conventional sense of the word. It is an elegant combination of a living museum and a working shop. Every exquisitely arranged cabinet holds Nikon treasures that I dreamed about as a child and those that I had the pleasure of owning. My first Nikon, a chrome FE2. The Nikon F2S Photomic and Nikon F3 given to me by my father. The Nikon FM3A and F100 I always wanted to have, and the memories of the 8mm Fisheye-Nikkor that gave me my first spherical images on 35mm film.

"One day I heard about Grays of Westminster and decided to visit. I wanted to ask whether I could get a lens serviced and the salesman told me that he would swap it for a new one. I explained that I bought the lens from somewhere else! He said that it would not be a problem, giving me a new lens in the famous gold box. First impressions last and this was my first encounter with the legendary service that Grays of Westminster is synonymous for. Soon afterwards, I became one of the founding subscribers of Nikon Owner magazine.

"On my next visit I bought two lenses and brought in some of my earliest panoramas to show, which due to their size, I had to lay onto the floor. By coincidence, Gray Levett had just walked into the showroom from his office and saw the pictures; he invited me to his office where he was being visited by Nikon U.K.'s Japanese MD who remarked, 'You took these pictures with a Nikon Coolpix?!'

"From that day our friendship and working relationship grew, and nearly ten years later, I have followed my passion and, with a similar work ethic to Gray's colleagues and staff, have organised nearly one hundred events for Nikon Owner, trained hundreds of subscribers and written numerous articles for Nikon Owner magazine. So it would be fair to say that the visit to Grays of Westminster that day was a life-changing moment!"

– Michael Eleftheriades
AA Dipl.

CHAPTER 7
ROCK MUSIC & PHOTOGRAPHY

Bob Dylan had predicted in February 1964, *"...you better start swimmin' or you'll sink like a stone/For the times they are a-changin'."*

At the time not everyone had anticipated the tidal wave of new ideas, beliefs and socio-ideological convictions that would occur during the nineteen-sixties and 'seventies, or the radical shift of perspective not just in thought and mind, but in almost every aspect of life and living.

This was no gentle evolution. Many long-established values had been assessed, found wanting and swallowed up in the engulfing current. Some people were active participants in the changes that occurred; others felt as if they should wait on the sidelines for some part of history to unfold that would make more sense than the present.

As with the relentless tide of any unexpected storm, cleansing and scourging as it moves forward, a tangle of debris was carried in its wake. The fragmented social mores from the nineteen-fifties that remained were sometimes held onto, perhaps precariously, by a few, as if they were the exhausted survivors from a foundered vessel clutching wildly at any flotsam or driftwood they could find floating in the backwash. And so it happened that the opposing ideologies of different generations were on occasion able to co-exist and co-inhabit the same arena to mutual benefit.

Gray Levett's very first job in the photographic world in his late teens was at N. Hartle Photographic in Bournemouth. The proprietor was not only very knowledgeable in the area of cameras and photography, but possessed an old-fashioned psyche that pursued with absolute conviction the concept

> "FOR GRAY, THE REBEL AND IDEALIST, THIS WAS INITIALLY A HARD BULLET TO BITE, BUT EVENTUALLY IT BECAME AS MUCH AN APPRENTICESHIP IN SUCCESSFULLY DEALING WITH CLIENTS...

N. Hartle Photographic,
Bournemouth circa 1966

of using the traditional methods of dealing with customers from the more deferential age of the nineteen-forties. He worked like an old commander himself and put his staff through a similar regime, involving them daily in cleaning, dusting, and presentation, as well as making sure the clientele were treated with respect and given extremely good service. For Gray, the rebel and idealist, this was initially a hard bullet to bite, but eventually it became as much an apprenticeship in successfully dealing with clients, as learning about the technical intricacies of film and camera. It would stand him in good stead for the future.

Gray at KJP (Keith Johnson Photographic)

Gray said, *"A few year later, after I had decided to move to London in order to broaden my career, something unexpected happened. I selected what I considered to be the best camera shop to work at based in central London. I was interviewed by the owner, another formidable figure. He questioned me intensively and at length. My responses were immediate, confident and without hesitation. Then it dawned on me; all the studying of photographic nomenclature, all the drilling on the key elements of dealing with people and all the months of training on how to provide a truly professional service fell into place. All those facts, all that study and drilling had become my own to use. I suddenly realised that my old boss, Mr Hartle, had given me something of great value. He had trained me to become competent and confident in my profession.*

"It was a moment of revelation to me. I learnt that you have to be a professional in whatever you do in life if you are to succeed.

"If you know your subject and can think with the information and have manual dexterity with your equipment, any professional in that field will recognize you as a professional too, but far more importantly, your knowledgeable professionalism will communicate to the customers with whom you are dealing and you will be listened to."

Early on in his career, Gray had made the conscious decision to work in as many different photographic environments as possible in order to broaden his experience in the photographic trade.

He considered that spending time being trained in smaller independent outlets, photographic companies that had a chain of stores and professional specialist photographic equipment shops would increase his understanding of how the photographic business worked as a whole. It would also give him access to and a working knowledge of the major cameras from the 16mm sub-minature Minox Camera to all the 35mm SLR systems as well as medium and large format.

From 1970 until 1977, Gray worked for a number of camera stores, including the London Camera Exchange Group, first of all at their Winchester Head Office, then at their Bournemouth branch, Fox Talbot in London, Keith Johnson Photographic, a large professional photographic dealer based in Ramillies Street, London (later to be acquired by Calumet Photographic) and Leslie S. Miller Photographic.

Gray at Leslie S. Miller Photographic

The erosion of the world of post-war Britain and its clash with the widespread changes during the nineteen-seventies had also begun to have an effect on consumerism. Familiar corner bakeries, greengroceries with their leafy carrots and earthy sacks of produce, old-fashioned sweet-shops, jars brimming with sherbet lemons and pear drops: all were beginning to be swallowed up by large conglomerates. The marketplace was re-inventing itself. Old-fashioned pharmacies and their tiny photographic departments which offered a developing and printing service were also gradually being inched out of the race by larger chains of chemists.

Leslie S. Miller Photographic was one of the companies that had circumnavigated this inevitable take-over, emerging successfully from its former incarnation as a pharmacy with a very small photographic department to become a business that sold purely precision photographic equipment. When Gray joined their team with manager Peter Walnes and another young assistant, Robert White (who went on to found Robert White Photographic), he started to deal with the ever-increasing professional market and a wide range of brands and formats of camera systems, including Nikon. By the time he moved on to work for other photographic outlets, Gray's appreciation of the developing Nikon system was already established.

Although the revolutionist ideology of the time had ignited a spontaneous energy in almost everyone who lived through the period, not every rebellion was anarchical or destructive. The transformation in popular thinking that saturated the politics of the late nineteen-sixties and 'seventies had simultaneously lit the beacon of a humanist and artistic renaissance whose bright idealism illuminated everything, and whether expressed through the medium of art, photography, writing or music, or a synthesis of all four, the mood was highly creative.

FOX TALBOT
179 Tottenham Court Road, London W.1.
01·636 1017

Nikon
DISCOUNT PRICE LIST MAY 1975

FOX TALBOT LTD, 179 TOTTENHAM COURT ROAD, LONDON W1. 01

"No.1 Shop for the Nikon Man".

We normally keep in stock all equipment listed here except for items shown in light type, which are obtained to special order.

Where prices are marked with a ... equipment is new and not yet a... stock, and the price is an estima...

NIKON F2

Nikon F2, f2 NF Nikkor	£246.00
Nikon F2, f1.4 NF Nikkor	£285.00
Nikon F2, 55mm Micro Nikkor	£281.00
Nikon F2 body	£187.50
Nikon Photomic F2, f2 NF Nikkor	£298.50
Nikon Photomic F2, f1.4 NF Nikkor	£337.50
Nikon Photomic F2, 55mm Micro	£333.50
Nikon Photomic F2 body	£240.00
Nikon Photomic F2S, f2 NF Nikkor	£337.50
Nikon Photomic F2S, f1.4 NF Nikkor	£376.50
Nikon Photomic F2S, 55mm Micro	£372.50
Nikon Photomic F2S body	£279.00
CH-1 Hard Case for Nikon F2	*£16.50*
CF-1 Semi-soft Case for Nikon F2	*£14.50*

Nikon F2 models are manufactured only with the Type A split image focussing screen, but on a new camera we will exchange this for any other screen listed for an extra charge of £6.00

NIKON MOVIE CAMERAS

R8 Super 8 Zoom
R10 Super 8 Zoom
EH-1 Compartment Case for R8
EF-2 Soft Case for R8
EF-1 Soft Case for R10
HR-2 Rubber Lens Hood for R
HR-3 Rubber Lens Hood for R
ES-2 Slide Copier for R8
ES-3 Slide Copier for R10
EA-1 Remote Control for R8
EA-2 Tape Recording Cord
EC-1 Close-up Lens for R8
EC-2 Close-up Lens for R10
EM-1 Microscope Adaptor fo

NIKKOR LENSES

Nikkor 15mm f5.6 & case
Nikkor 18mm f4 & case
Nikkor 20mm f4
Nikkor 24mm f2.8
Nikkor 28mm f2

Gray's involvement with photography and camera equipment had evolved side by side with an increasing interest in the Blues and Rock bands of the time.

Using black & white film as a medium, Gray shot photographs of many of the bands that played at The Ritz, a low bow-windowed 1950's ballroom in Bournemouth, such as Black Sabbath on their first tour of England with Ozzy Osbourne, Jethro Tull, the original Fleetwood Mac with legendary guitarist Peter Green, The Nice, with keyboard virtuoso Keith Emerson (later of Emerson, Lake and Palmer) and a dazzling array of some of the hottest names from the music explosion of the period, including Rod Stewart. Gray had originally been introduced to Rod Stewart by Don Shinn, the keyboard player of the Southampton band The Soul Agents, during his mid-teens. Rod had smuggled Gray into a gig at Le Disque a Go! Go! telling the doorman that he was a roadie, an unlikely explanation as Gray was wearing school uniform at the time. Gray was to meet Rod Stewart again some years later when he paid a visit to Grays of Westminster with Penny Lancaster, who had been a customer of Grays while she was studying photography.

Keith Emerson and The Nice

Gray also started a band of his own in the nineteen-seventies, called When Stars Collide, playing the flute and writing all of the lyrics. The members of the group included his late wife Malenie Schofield who had been part of Stone Monkey, the dance troupe attached to The Incredible String Band, an exceptionally creative and influential band of the nineteen-sixties and early nineteen-seventies which Gray also had close ties with.

Rod Stewart & The Soul Agents

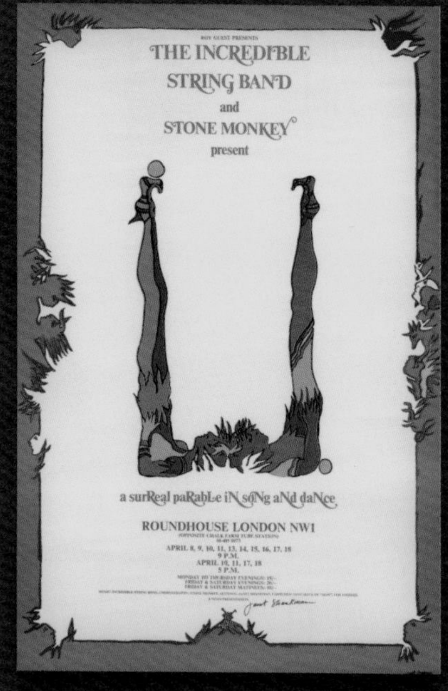

Left: Gray Levett with Robin Williamson, co-founder of The Incredible String Band.

Above: U poster for The Incredible String Band and Stone Monkey

Opposite page top: Kate Bush

Opposite page bottom right: Glen Row, Scottish Borders

The other members of When Stars Collide were talented musicians and singers such as Jon Bavin, who went on to work with the Eurythmics, Bob Geldof and Bob Dylan, a pianist called Rivers Pound, the multi-talented Justin Robertson on lead guitar and drummer John Gilston, who later worked with Donna Summer, Stanley Clarke and Earth Wind & Fire. Gray was involved in the promotion of the band as well.

A short while before *Wuthering Heights* became a Number 1 hit record, the inspirational English singer-songwriter, musician and record-producer Kate Bush was a weekend guest at Gray and Malenie's home near the sea in Dorset. Gray said, "*Over the course of that summer weekend we talked about her desire to make it in the music business and she played the piano in my sitting room. I asked her if she had a demo tape with her and was simply held spellbound by what I heard; not only was her voice potent and beautifully strange, but the songs were hauntingly memorable, unlike anything I had ever heard. We stayed in touch and a few years later when Wuthering Heights became universally well-known, some of the songs on that demo tape would go on to form part of her first album The Kick Inside.*"

In the late nineteen-seventies, now working independently in the photographic business, Gray moved to a remote cottage in the Scottish Borders with Malenie.

However, in 1979 Malenie tragically died of cancer and Gray was invited to Los Angeles by some close friends to recover from his loss. He decided to stay over there for a while.

Speaking to Gray about those days, he said, *"It was a very difficult period of my life. I was in my very early thirties and had just experienced a deeply personal and unexpected tragedy. I was in new, unfamiliar territory, both emotionally and physically. I also had to pull myself together very quickly; my savings had evaporated all too soon and I had to take a number of jobs just to make ends meet, such as gardening or working in a Mexican sweatshop."*

"WE STAYED IN TOUCH AND A FEW YEARS LATER WHEN *WUTHERING HEIGHTS* BECAME UNIVERSALLY WELL-KNOWN, SOME OF THE SONGS ON THAT DEMO TAPE WOULD GO ON TO FORM PART OF HER FIRST ALBUM *THE KICK INSIDE*."

Eventually, Gray did find his feet, and started working on the pilot for a radio show called *The Other Side of Hollywood* with American comedian and scriptwriter John Settle.

Shortly afterwards, he got together with Forrest J Ackerman, the celebrated science-fiction literary agent, who had introduced the science fiction and fantasy genre to a generation of young readers through the *Famous Monsters of Filmland Magazine.* Ackerman had spent a lifetime amassing what was probably, at the time, the world's largest personal collection of science-fiction/fantasy memorabilia. He provided inspiration to many who would later become successful artists, writers or directors, such as Peter Jackson, Steven Spielberg, Tim Burton, Stephen King and George Lucas.

Gray and Forrest J Ackerman, Chicago

It was through Forrest that Gray met Ray Bradbury, one of the most celebrated American writers of the 20th century. Ray Bradbury is best-known for his dystopian novel *Fahrenheit 451*, as well as *The Martian Chronicles* and *The Illustrated Man*. Forrest also introduced Gray to George Clayton Johnson, an American science-fiction writer most famous for co-writing the novel *Logan's Run* with William F. Nolan and well-known for his work in television, writing screenplays for such notable series as *The Twilight Zone* and *Star Trek*. He also wrote the story on which the 1960 and later 2001 film, *Ocean's Eleven* was based.

Gray was delighted when he discovered that the September 1982 issue of *Famous Monsters of Filmland* magazine had been dedicated to him.

Gray said, *"Forrest J Ackerman was a great lover of puns, and was affectionately known as 4E or Forry. One time we had our photograph taken together, which later I discovered framed on the wall of his museum. The caption read: The Picture of Forry and Gray[4]."*

In late October 1982 the Mayor of Los Angeles Tom Bradley announced in a press release that he would accept Forrest J Ackerman's multi-million dollar science fiction collection numbering over 300,000 pieces. A Science Fiction Museum Committee was formed; its members included Ray Bradbury, Harlan Ellison, Vincent Price, Gene Roddenberry (creator of Star Trek), Steven Spielberg and many others. Much to his surprise Gray Levett was also elected to be a member of this august committee.

Whilst in LA, Gray continued to maintain strong ties with the U.K. as the American correspondent for *ADASTRA*, a British science-fiction/science-fact magazine, and also wrote a column for Kate Bush in the *Kate Bush Magazine*, covering the U.S. perspective on her career; she kindly agreed to do an interview with *The Other Side of Hollywood* radio show, as well as a voice-trailer for them.

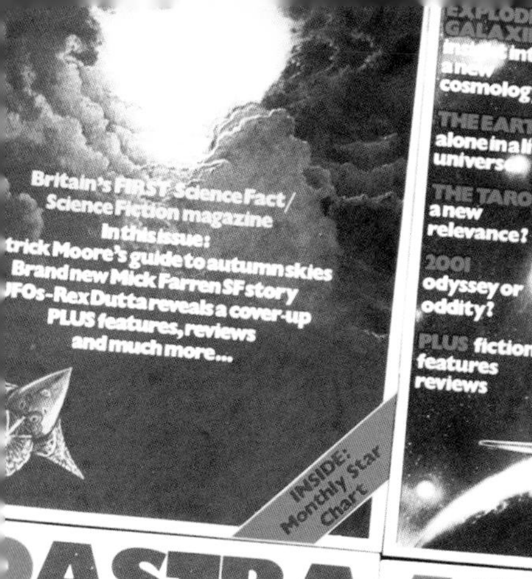

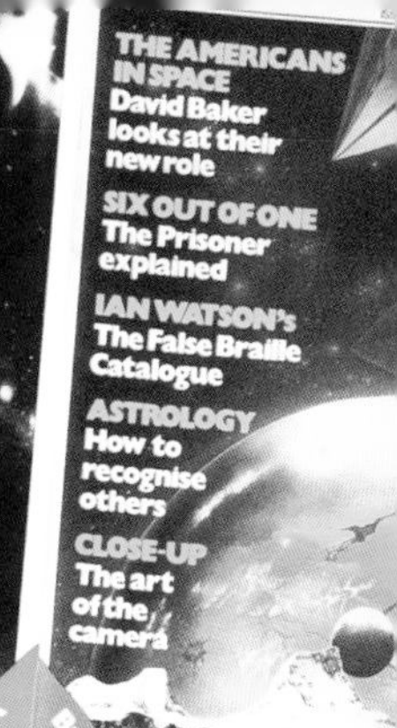

OFFICE OF THE MAYOR

TOM BRADLEY
MAYOR

CITY HALL
...NGELES, CALIFORNIA 90012
(213) 485-3311

October 13, 1982

...r. Gray Levett
...riton Books
. O. Box 27461
...os Angeles, California 90027

...ear Mr. Levett:

The day has arrived!

On October 21, at 10 a.m., in Room 305, City Hall, Mayor's Conference Room, the largest collection of Sci-Fi memorabilia and books will be officially donated to the City of Los Angeles by Forrest Ackerman.

You are invited to the first meeting of the Sci-Fi Museum Committee immediately after the press conference in Room 305, Mayor's Conference Room.

I believe this is a significant day for the City of Los Angeles and hope you will be with us to start planning a major museum which will house and exhibit the collection.

Please RSVP to Frances Ambrozich at 485-5102.

Sincerely,

Tom Bradley

TOM BRADLEY
Mayor

TB/fa

“I WOULD BE BUYING AND SELLING CAMERAS FROM MY SISTER’S KITCHEN IN THE EVENING, THEN TEARING OFF IN A TAXI TO MEET WITH SOMEONE LIKE ART GARFUNKEL TO DISCUSS A …TURE U.K. OR EUROPEAN

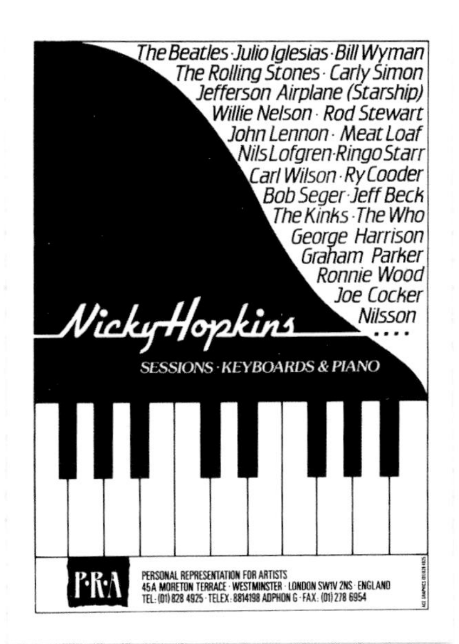

But five years on, the initial excitement of the perpetual blue skies and lifestyle of 'Tinseltown' was wearing thin and Gray was singularly homesick. He was haunted by an unrequited desire for all that was British: green grass, strong tea, umbrellas, grey skies and the perpetual drizzle that seems to paradoxically both dampen and soothe the spirit. A letter from his sister Susie, the late celebrated artist and writer and the lost pleasure of a walk beside the Thames in spring and English afternoon tea served in thin china cups at Fortnum & Mason finally precipitated Gray's return to the U.K. in 1984.

Shortly afterwards, he was offered the opportunity to run the promotions department of an Indie record label at their recording studios near Chalk Farm in London, which involved press launches and attending gigs. In the months that followed, Gray also formed his own company, PRA, Personal Representation For Artists, after he was independently approached to act as personal manager to Rock's greatest session man, the legendary piano-player Nicky Hopkins. Nicky's work had graced landmark songs by the Rolling Stones, The Beatles, The Who, Jeff Beck and Rod Stewart.

Long gone was the photographer of yesteryear, mixing his potions and inky chemicals to the mutterings of mystical incantations in the dark room. Long gone too, were the Fleet Street men, smelling of hypo and pungent with nicotine, wielding their plate cameras, hands permanently stained brown from being immersed in developer. Photography and photographic equipment had taken a new turn, a new momentum, and the future was auspicious.

After a chance conversation with Gray's one-time employer, Peter Walnes, the former manager of Leslie S. Miller Photographic, it seemed that it might be just the right moment to start a small camera company, albeit initially from his sister's home, one that would specifically deal in mail-order.

"In those very early days," Gray said, *"I would be buying and selling cameras from my sister's kitchen in the evening, then tearing off in a taxi to meet with someone like Art Garfunkel to discuss a future U.K. or European tour with Nicky Hopkins."*

Art Garfunkel, Gray Levett and Nicky Hopkins

But Gray's interest in photography had not waned during his time in America, and, perhaps first of all out of curiosity, he started to research the current photographic trade and the changes that had occurred since he had been actively part of it some years before.

Gray finally handed in his notice to the Indie record label, and then, when his client Nicky Hopkins moved to America to live, he decided to concentrate all his energies on developing and expanding his newly formed camera business in Pimlico, Westminster.

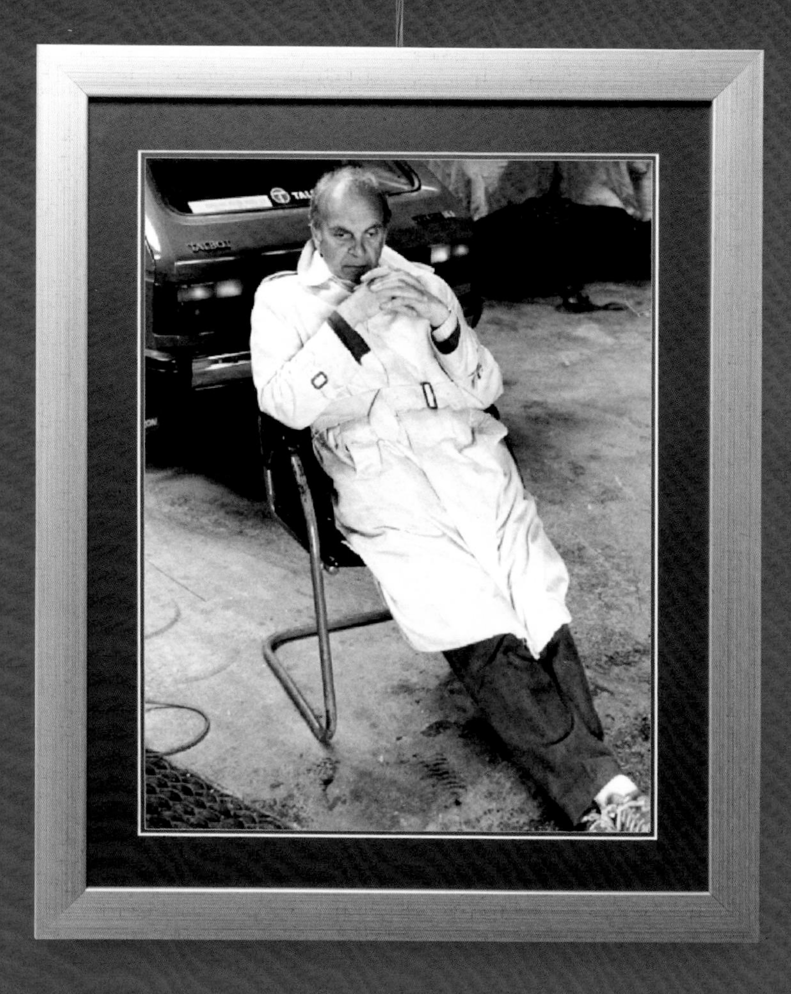

JOHN KRISH

John Krish, writer, editor and director of both features and documentary films, started his career in the early part of the Second World War as an assistant to directors and editors in the GPO Film Unit that became the Crown Film Unit.

With such a thorough apprenticeship he was to develop into a writer and director whose work ranged from science fiction, *Unearthly Stranger* to sophisticated British comedy, *Decline and Fall*. His television work included *The Avengers* (starring Patrick Macnee and Diana Rigg) and many familiar commercials.

Recently his long career in British documentary has come to the notice of the critics who described him as the master of post-war documentary film-making and the compilation, *A Day in the Life* with four of his deeply-felt films was given *The Evening Standard* Award for Best Documentary.

“Straight off, Churton Street is the wrong address. Where should they be, I hear you ask? The answer is obvious, Harley Street. With the kind of specialist care and advice that is Grays of Westminster’s hallmark, there should be a waiting room with old copies of Punch and Country Life.

“On a serious note, one doesn’t just shop at Grays of Westminster, you’re made welcome and served by people who know and care equally for the Nikon product and their valued customers. And whether you’re buying a filter or the latest camera body, the help and courtesy will be at the same high and all too rare level.

“This extraordinary mixture of kindness and knowledge puts every other shop, camera or otherwise, to shame.”

– John Krish

CHAPTER 8
THEY CAME TO SW1

The London postal address SW1 of which Grays of Westminster is famously part, has seen the rise and fall, occasionally the births and deaths, of many celebrated and varied inhabitants: poets, writers, politicians and composers.

The list is full and contains such luminaries such as Sir Isaac Newton, (1642-1727), poet Alfred Lord Tennyson, (1809-1892), Joseph Conrad the novelist and Ian Fleming, the creator of James Bond, who lived at 22 Ebury Street, SW1. Wolfgang Amadeus Mozart (1756-1791) composed his first symphony in 180 Ebury Street in 1764, Henry Purcell lived in Old Pye Street, SW1, and in 1848 Frederic Chopin (1810-1849) went to the Guildhall from 4 St James's Place, SW1 to give his last public performance.

SW1's collection of famous live-in politicians includes Nancy Astor, the first woman to sit in Parliament and several celebrated prime ministers such as Robert Walpole, Stanley Baldwin and Lady Margaret Thatcher. But perhaps the most celebrated statesman of them all was Sir Winston Churchill, who first lived at 33 Eccleston Square and then later in Morpeth Terrace, SW1.

Not far from Grays of Westminster, at the southern end of St George's Drive and Denbigh Street, stands a statue of the patron saint of Pimlico architecture, Thomas Cubitt (1788-1855) by the artist William Fawke. It was Cubitt who created the graceful architectural simplicity that is the embodiment of Pimlico today. The figure, contemplatively vigilant, is caught between thought and action, midway between the vision of an idea and the constant creation of work in progress.

E CONSTITUTION
HENEKEYS LTD
ESTD 1695
42
BARBER SHOP
HAIRCUTTING
BRYLCREEM
CHURTON ST.
CHURTO

Churton Street circa 1940s
showing Whites Barbers

Thomas Cubitt
Gardens
Marylebone
Edgware Rd Stat.
Russell Squ.
Bedford Squ.
Nat. Gallery
Trafalgar Squ.
Admiralty
St James's Park
Buckingham Pal.
Belgrave Squ.
BROMPTON
S. Kensington Stat.
W E S T M I N S T E R
Westminst. Abbey
Hse. of Parliament
Victoria Stat.
Vincent Square
Lambeth Br.
P I M L I C O
Nat. Gallery of Brit. Art
Chelsea Hosp.
Barracks
C H E L S E A
Grosvenor Rd Stat.
Vauxhall Br.
T H A M E S
Chelsea Embankment
Battersea
Southwark u Vauxhall Water Works
Gas Works
Albert Embankment

Looking at the present day Pimlico with its white classical townhouses, its wide, sweeping vistas and elegant garden squares, it is hard to imagine that before development, the area was weeded and cropped by market gardeners and filled with osier beds[5]. Low-lying, marshy and prone to flooding, some parts had an almost fen-like desolation about them. Its earlier inhabitants too had links to a more notorious past. As far back as the Peasants' Revolt in 1381, rebels gathered in the area to make their own statement against authority. In the next century, a famous witch, Margerie Gourdemaine, resided somewhere in the surrounding marshes brewing her 'medecines and drinkes'.

The origin of the word 'Pimlico' has itself caused interest and speculation. It is possible that the word derives from a Ben Pimlico, a publican of the Tudor times, or even from the Spanish word 'pimplar', meaning to 'drink to excess'. In the early part of the seventeenth century much serious drinking was attributed to Pimlico.

With the building of the Royal Hospital in the latter part of the seventeenth century and the opening of Ranelagh Gardens in 1733, the area began to thrive, but it was Thomas Cubitt who changed the face of the area.

From humble beginnings, born in the village of Buxton, Norfolk in 1788, he rose to take his place alongside the most distinguished of Victorian achievers. He was well-known for his philanthropic works and received the patronage of royalty. As a master builder who revolutionised the construction industry, he left an elegant legacy of buildings, many of which are still standing in the twenty-first century.

During the eighteen-forties, the raising of Pimlico went on at a rapid pace. Cubitt's diagonal 'grid' plan in Pimlico gave an apparency that the area was an extension of Belgravia, which itself was fast becoming a very sought-after place to live in.

The house style was set by Cubitt himself but influenced to a degree by the second Marquess of Westminster, who was very keen on the terrace, stucco and the balcony-over-doric-portico style characteristic of Pimlico houses. The architectural style of 'Italianate-Westminster Portico', and the layout of the streets themselves inspired the feeling of gracious boulevards and visual spaciousness.

By the time he died in 1855, he had created, from an original site of desolate marshland, the Pimlico we are familiar with today.

The years following saw the transformation of Battersea fields to a public park, the building of St. Saviour's Church in St. George's Square and St. Barnabas' in Pimlico Road (attended by the celebrated artist Aubrey Beardsley who lived nearby). The main shopping areas were created in Lupus Street and in Warwick Way. Street markets, to the distaste of many Victorian residents, could be found in Churton Street,

> “AN ANONYMOUS WRITER WROTE OF PIMLICO IN 1877: *“THIS IS THE ABODE OF GENTILITY – A SERVANT OR TWO IN THE KITCHEN, BIRDS IN THE WINDOWS, WITH FLOWERS IN BOXES, PIANOS, AND THE LATEST FASHIONS”.*

Moreton Street and Warwick Way. The Warwick Way market survived until the end of the Second World War when it moved into the top part of Tachbrook Street and corner of Churton Street where it now stands.

An anonymous writer wrote of Pimlico in 1877: *"This is the abode of gentility – a servant or two in the kitchen, birds in the windows, with flowers in boxes, pianos, and the latest fashions".*

But, by the time 1914 arrived, although the majority of the population was eminently genteel, some parts of Pimlico were beginning to suffer from overcrowding.

Pimlico was one of several parts of London to be bombed during the First World War, and the post-war period created a demand for more housing and better living conditions. When the River Thames burst its banks in 1928, catastrophic flooding resulted, and the scale of Pimlico's housing problem made national news and brought the matter to national attention. Many new flats were built between 1929 and 1938 in Pimlico, and the late Queen Mother was given a tour of its various successful housing schemes.

At the top end of the market, Dolphin Square, the largest block of luxury flats in Europe to date, was also constructed: two thousand luxury flats complete with a shopping area, restaurant, swimming pool and ballroom.

But the Second World War bombing of 1940, 1941 and 1944 brought devastation and chaos to Pimlico, although Cubitt's sturdily-built coal cellars were converted by the Council into shelters. An entire street, Pimlico's oldest pub, and a factory in Grosvenor Road were all destroyed in one raid. Another time, part of a nearby railway line was blown up and large pieces of railway fell like a brutal hailstorm all over Pimlico. Morale was nevertheless high. Miss Rose Capone, at the time the proprietress of Churton Tea Rooms at 42 Churton Street, was serving a customer breakfast when the lintel holding up the frontage of the building collapsed and glass was blown straight off her front window. She and her brother calmly cleared it up and continued to serve hot tea and toast in the rubble around them.

From the end of the war and through the nineteen-fifties, the inhabitants of Pimlico were beginning to earn a reputation as a close community, a congruous people who were mutually supportive yet highly individualistic at the same time.

The black & white film *Innocent Sinners*, a gentle children's drama based on the novel *An Episode of Sparrows* by Rumer Godden, following a young girl's frustrated efforts to brighten her drab life during the period of post-war austerity by cultivating a bomb-site garden, touches on this theme. It starred Dame Flora Robson, and was largely filmed in Churton Street.

Likewise, when the famous Ealing comedy *Passport to Pimlico*, starring Stanley Holloway and Margaret Rutherford, was released in the Spring of 1949, the film was easily believable as an expression of all that was paradoxical and idiosyncratic about the British.

By 1985, the year Gray Levett founded Grays of Westminster, most of Pimlico had already been vastly renovated and gentrified and the vision of Cubitt's dream with its uncluttered elegance and wide roadways had been restored from the classical vistas of St George's Drive and Belgrave Road to the elegant Georgian simplicity of Warwick Square. ■

THE RANK ORGANISATION PRESENTS

INNOCENT SINNERS

STANLEY KUBRICK

The late Stanley Kubrick was an American film director, screenwriter, producer, cinematographer, editor and photographer. Kubrick's films are considered by many to be among the most important contributions to world cinema in the twentieth century, and he is frequently quoted as being one of the greatest and most influential directors of all time.

Kubrick was a perfectionist and assumed control over most aspects of the filmmaking process, taking immense care with research, scene-staging and camera-work. The cinematography in many of Kubrick's films was highly innovative at the time, such as *2001: A Space Odyssey* (1968), a science-fiction film with powerful visual effects. It earned him an Oscar and Steven Spielberg referred to the film as his generation's 'big bang'; it regularly tops the charts of the greatest films ever made. Many of his other films were nominated for Oscars, Golden Globes or BAFTAs. His films have included *Eyes Wide Shut, Full Metal Jacket, The Shining, Barry Lyndon, A Clockwork Orange, 2001: A Space Odyssey, Dr. Strangelove or: How I Learned to Stop Worrying and Love the Bomb, Lolita, Spartacus, Paths of Glory, The Killing, Killer's Kiss*. In 2000, BAFTA renamed their Britannia lifetime achievement award the 'Stanley Kubrick Britannia Award'.

"Stanley Kubrick left school in the mid-1940s and became a professional photographer for Look magazine. In fact, as a teenager, he was the youngest staff photographer the magazine ever employed. He began with a plate camera and then moved on to the 6 x 6cm format.

"In the early 1950s he moved over to 35mm SLR cameras and never looked back. He probably had more cameras than shirts and though he sometimes dallied with other makes Nikon was always his preferred system.

"I only ever knew him to defer to two people on matters photographic: Geoffrey Crawley, one time editor of the BJP, and Gray Levett and the Grays of Westminster gang down in Pimlico who continue to give us an unrivalled service".*

– Tony Frewin
Personal Assistant to Stanley Kubrick
Estate of Stanley Kubrick

*BJP: British Journal of Photography

CHAPTER 9
THE GAMBLE

Like many extremely successful businessmen before and afterwards, Gray Levett started the newly formed company with absolutely no stock, little wherewithal, but plenty of guts.

He scraped together one hundred pounds and placed tiny, inexpensive advertisements in the classified section of *Amateur Photographer* magazine. The harsh actuality was that he had very little equipment to sell in the early days, and it was Peter Walnes, Gray's one-time employer, who gave him his first line of credit, as well as supplying a range and variety of second-hand equipment which he then sold on.

It was an interesting initiation. In the first one or two weeks, the phones only rang a couple of times a day, but Gray used the time to study and research the second-hand photographic market in depth until he eventually made enough sales to give the business a formal kick start. He had a tiny room, no money, no cameras and an old door turned into a desk, supported either end by two red filing cabinets, a couple of chairs and a telephone.

The newly-formed company was initially called simply Grays, but Gray instinctively felt it was important to position the name with a location, so it ultimately became Grays of Westminster. With the combination of almost non-existent overheads and a dedicated mixture of flair, determination and Gray's prior photographic know-how, little by little the business built up a steady clientele. He continued to take out advertisements in

SHOP & PREMISES
TO LET
DAUNTONS
834 8000

40

WHITES BARBERS
HAIRCUTTING
for WELL GROOMED HAIR
Vaseline HAIR TONIC
Checks DRY SCALP
GENTS SALOON

the classified section of *Amateur Photographer* magazine and steadily made good progress, doing more and more buying and selling.

Although he was dealing within the second-hand bracket of bodies and lenses, he was nevertheless convinced that they should stick to good quality equipment and sold the top brands in 35mm, such as Nikon, Canon, Minolta, Pentax, some Leica, medium format Hasselblad, Mamiya and Bronica.

" ... IT BECAME IMPERATIVE TO CONSIDER MOVING INTO SHOP PREMISES TO ACCOMMODATE THE EXPANDING BUSINESS.

For photographers trying to purchase second-hand equipment in the UK during that time, the market was often fraught with barriers, obstacles and the occasional landmine. Most second-hand bodies or lenses for sale were listed in laboriously long columns, with little clear delineation apart from the name of the company, the hours of business and the telephone number followed by frequently ill-defined lists of equipment with sub-headings. It was often a hazardous exercise for the photographer attempting to purchase used equipment, filled with unease and disappointment. Furthermore, the definitions of the description of the camera or lens were often blurred and the distinctions of cosmetic quality unclear. The equipment would be labelled as good, very good, as new, like new, and these relied precariously on opinion rather than exact scientific categorisation.

In his own camera business, Peter Walnes had further developed a method of equipment grading in the UK, which he had imported from America from a company called Del's Camera Inc. in Santa Barbara. This equipment grading description was broken down into a number of categories: mint, mint minus, excellent plus plus, excellent plus, excellent and V.G.. Peter was the first person to use this system and in his own company he provided useful guarantees on second-hand equipment as well as a unique fourteen-day full money-back approval. This meant if a person was not satisfied with his purchase, he could return it for a full refund. This in itself allowed potential purchasers to buy with a certain amount of confidence; the grading of the equipment would also match the grading in the advertisement.

Gray decided to employ the same format of grading description and the same business procedures of guarantee on second-hand purchases as Peter Walnes. Having decided to endorse a certain standard for both the categorisation and marketing of equipment, Grays of Westminster's reputation for selling quality cameras began to grow and with this the company began to expand. The discreet mail-order company hitherto envisaged was soon changing out of all recognition, and the premises was brimming with equipment and sometimes the unexpected customer.

As customers became increasingly interested in visiting the company, it became imperative to consider moving into shop premises to accommodate the expanding business.

A vacant business property was eventually found, an old-fashioned hairdressers in Churton Street, Pimlico, called Whites Barbers. Furthermore, local legend had it that the same barbers had been used by Winston Churchill who had lived nearby during World War II. ■

DANIEL LEZANO

An enthusiast photographer for over 30 years, Daniel Lezano has long enjoyed a passion for photography, in particular portraits. During his career he has worked on some of the U.K.'s leading photography titles. Following three years on *Practical Photography* as technical writer/editor, he left to launch *Photography Monthly*, where he was editor until 2006.

He went on to co-found Halo Publishing and launch and edit *Digital SLR Photography*, the U.K.'s leading photo title for digital SLR users, which was later acquired by Dennis Publishing in 2008. Daniel is also the author of several best-selling photography books, including *The Photography Bible* and *100 Ways To Take Better Portrait Photographs.*

"Fuelled by the digital revolution, the photographic landscape has changed beyond all recognition over the last couple of decades. The one constant during this period has been Grays of Westminster, a camera store that has provided and maintained a unique and unrivalled level of service and expertise since it first opened its doors in 1985.

"I'm pretty confident that there is no other camera shop like Grays of Westminster, not just in London or the U.K., but also anywhere in the world. If you have ever visited this emporium of all things Nikon, then I'm sure you'll fully agree that it sets the standard on so many key levels. The extensive range of Nikon cameras, Nikkor lenses and accessories kept in stock is second-to-none, while the incredible inventory of used equipment marks it is as an Aladdin's cave for the collector.

"Even more impressive however, is the high level of expertise and service that Gray and his team provide their customers. I can't imagine anywhere else where technical queries or requirements for items new or old are better served than at Grays. It's of little surprise that it boasts the reputation it has and the multitude of awards that recognises the efforts made to provide photographers with the very best service. Grays of Westminster, like Nikon, represents quality at its best.

"Grays of Westminster has enjoyed many notable incredible achievements over the years and has earned the distinction as the nation's most respected camera store. The accolades are reward for the effort and dedication that Gray has provided for over a quarter of a century and I'm in no doubt this unique centre of excellence will continue to provide the finest service for decades to come."

– Daniel Lezano
Editor, Digital SLR Photography

CHAPTER 10
40 CHURTON STREET

Derek Cooke, a professional photographer and one of Grays of Westminster's earliest customers from 1985, met Gray Levett outside *Whites Barbers* for a tour of the building.

Derek explains, *"Gray invited me to London on a surprise visit, so I had no idea where we were going or what to expect. He said he had something interesting to show me. Having obtained various photographic publications from him over the time period, I was not at all surprised to receive a phone call from him and, with the anticipation of obtaining another publication, we arranged to meet. Standing outside 40 Churton Street, I waited while Gray found the right key to enter the premises. It was a building in a quiet street in Pimlico, an old barber shop full of rubbish and disregarded items, abandoned and in a state of complete disrepair. Walking a few yards down the corridor we entered the ground floor room. The sight before us was as if time had stopped in the 1950s. I remember looking at him questioningly; Gray had hesitated and then, with an unfathomable expression in his eyes, had explained that he was expanding the business and that this old barber shop fitted the bill. I remember saying to him in astonishment, 'Really! Are you sure?'"*

Gray was not perturbed by the extensive renovation that would be needed and decided to go ahead. Furthermore, as the whole building was in an extremely bad state of repair, Gray was able to use the opportunity to create an interior design from scratch to change *Whites Barbers* into Grays of Westminster.

When the renovation project progressed and the word got about that a new camera shop was opening in Westminster, Gray and his team looked at a number of proposals for the interior design.

Gray's vision was very clear and stemmed entirely from his basic reason for wanting to establish such a business in the first place: to endeavour to create the finest example of a photographic store unrivalled anywhere in the world.

It would be the embodiment of a place where customers would always be welcomed, have their questions fully answered and receive friendly and well-informed service; they would be able to purchase any piece of photographic equipment they needed quickly and efficiently and to do so in pleasurable and comfortable surroundings.

“WITH OAK-PANELLED WALLS, A RESTORED VICTORIAN FIREPLACE, RICH WOOL CARPETING, BRASS SUMMONING BELLS AND LEATHER-TOPPED DESKS INSTEAD OF COUNTERS, GRAY LEVETT CREATED THE VERY DISTINCTIVE INTERIOR DESIGN THAT WAS SINGULARLY GRAYS OF WESTMINSTER.

In essence, Gray wanted to create a calm, unhurried environment with an atmosphere of simple elegance, away from the bewildering tumult of commerce and merchandising, a haven of calm in which a customer could feel completely at ease.

Design features that might include walls painted in an inquisitorial white gloss, impersonal office furniture, laminated, wipe-clean counters or grey corporate carpeting were rejected, as was a lighting system so bright that a customer would feel both interrogated and intimidated into passive acquiescence.

The ubiquitous window display of many photographic outlets with their fluorescent price-tickets superimposed on a huddle of pick-and-mix second-hand equipment was also discarded.

The interior design would need to fit Gray’s concept of graceful simplicity and the template came in part from the design of the gentlemen’s clubs of Pall Mall in the early part of the nineteenth century.

The concept of the Gentlemen’s Club was very much that of a long-standing English institution, a place where like-minded men could meet. Many of the clubs had their origins in the coffee-houses that came into existence during the eighteenth century, and they were usually located in the SW1 areas of London, such as Pall Mall and St. James’s.

Henry James, the Bostonian novelist who moved to London in 1876, wrote *“There are winter effects, not intrinsically sweet, it would appear, which somehow, in absence, touch the chords of memory and even the fount of tears… as for instance… The interior glow of the clubs in Pall Mall.”*

Painting by
Kridon Panteli

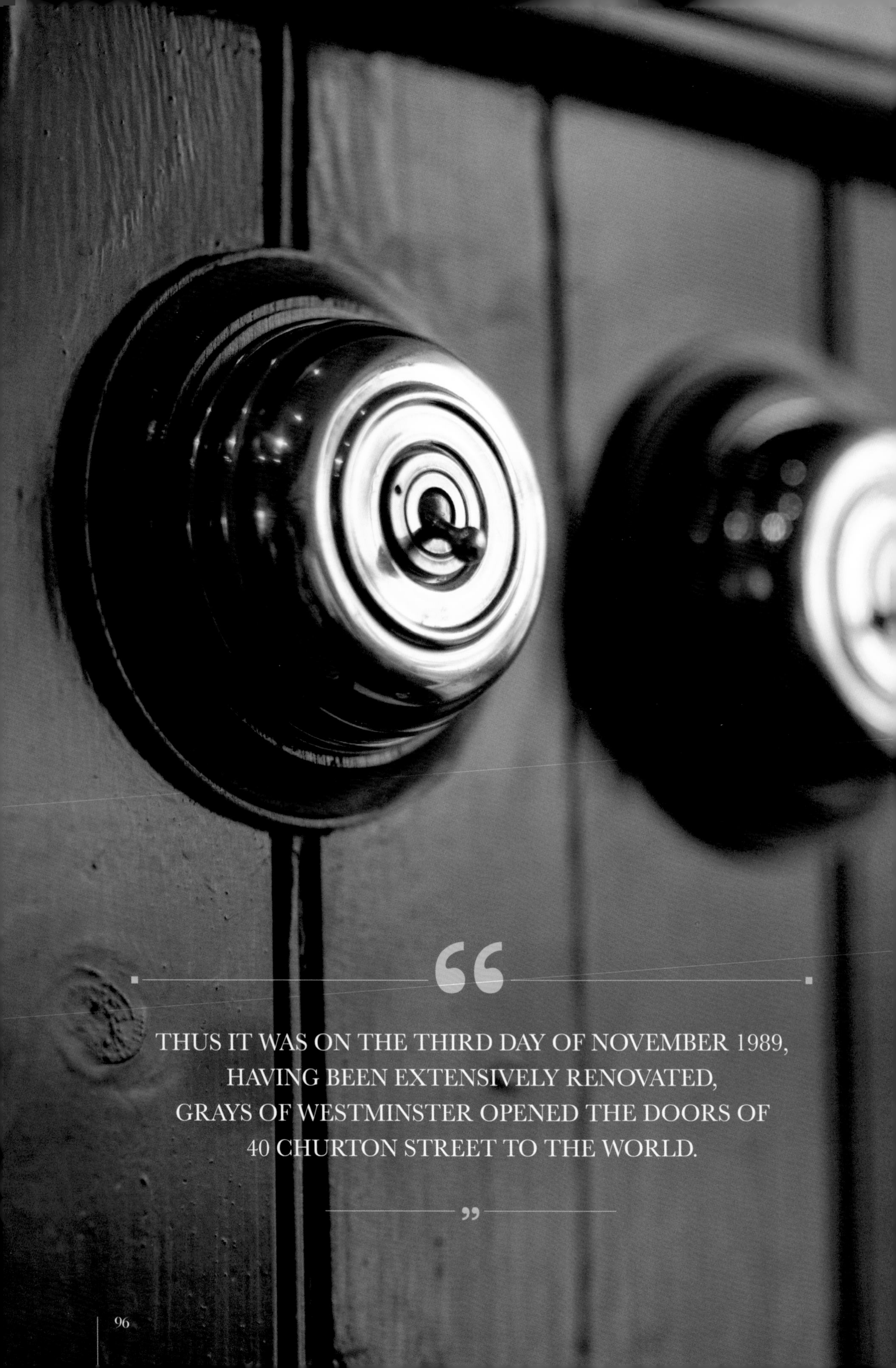

> "THUS IT WAS ON THE THIRD DAY OF NOVEMBER 1989, HAVING BEEN EXTENSIVELY RENOVATED, GRAYS OF WESTMINSTER OPENED THE DOORS OF 40 CHURTON STREET TO THE WORLD."

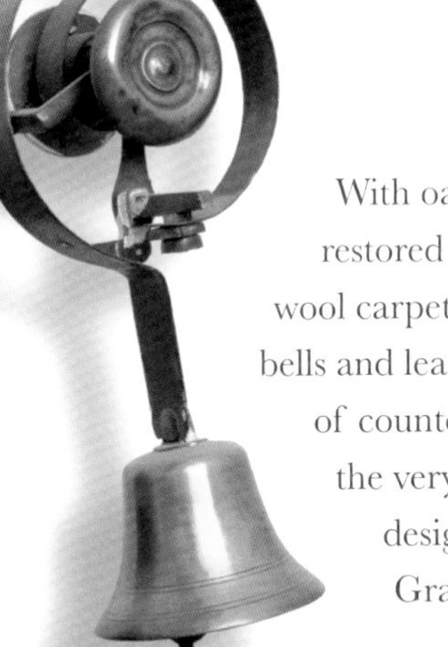

With oak-panelled walls, a restored Victorian fireplace, rich wool carpeting, brass summoning bells and leather-topped desks instead of counters, Gray Levett created the very distinctive interior design that was singularly Grays of Westminster.

Gray said, *"I wanted to have old-fashioned glass-fronted cabinets of dark wood with brass fittings and traditional leather-topped desks; I saw no reason why people should stand behind a counter and wait there while someone showed them an expensive piece of equipment. As with expensive jewellers, such as Asprey in New Bond Street, why shouldn't someone come in and sit down at ease with their surroundings to make their choices of equipment?"*

Likewise, he did not want an array of ill-sorted cameras with scribbled price tickets filling the window; instead, he preferred a simple display of fresh flowers or framed photographic images.

The distinctive company logo was inspired by the artistry of Victorian copperplate; Gray had a fine handwriting style himself and had always admired the style of copperplate.

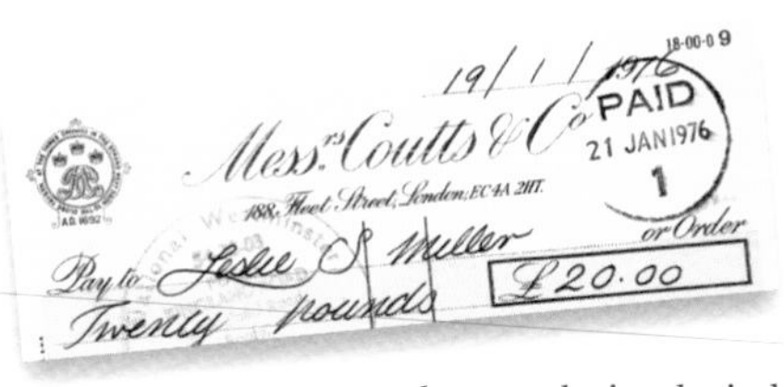

A small number of distinguished businesses had for many years retained a copperplate style in their logo such as the bankers Messrs. Coutts & Co., Messrs. Hoare & Co. and Messrs. Drummond; Gray wanted the company image to reflect this concept of old-fashioned, knowledgeable service. The Grays of Westminster logo was designed by a young graphic artist by the name of Alan Evans.

The emphasis on both the logo and the design of the interior of the shop was in essence a physical manifestation of the attention to detail for which Grays of Westminster was already becoming legendary.

Thus it was on the third day of November 1989, having been extensively renovated, Grays of Westminster opened the doors of 40 Churton Street to the world.

And, as if by some twist of fate that strangely concurred with the legacy of elegant gentility of the early part of the twentieth century that they were at pains to re-create, the high-tech phone system that had been ordered failed to arrive on time. For a few days after Grays opened, the staff were forced instead to use heavy black Bakelite telephones with strident ringing tones from the nineteen-forties. ■

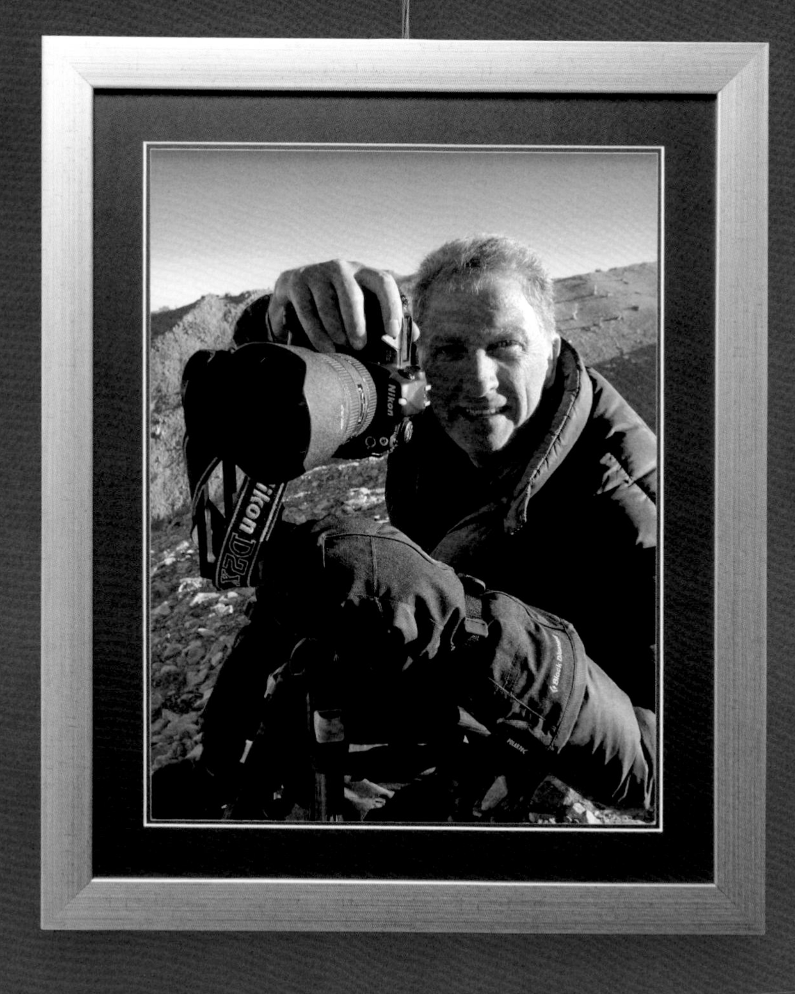

NEIL LUCAS

Neil Lucas was a producer with the BBC's world renowned Natural History Unit for over 20 years. During that time he worked on many international award-winning productions, including Sir David Attenborough's *Trials of Life, The Private Life of Plants, The Life of Mammals, Planet Earth* and the highly acclaimed *Life* series.

Many of Neil's programmes and productions were the most technically challenging to have ever been made, and were nominated for many International, BAFTA and EMMY awards.

Neil now works as a freelance film director, producer and photographer specializing in the more demanding and technical shoots.
He works alongside some of the world's top photographers and film makers, using new and state of the art filming and photographic techniques, many of which he is recognised worldwide. www.lucasproductions.com

"It's not every day you discover a small shop that completely overwhelms your senses. But as soon as you approach that blue front door you instantly start to smile. This happily continues as you step over the threshold, and enter a truly unique and magical world which could quite easily belong to a period drama.

"It would be a period drama with a difference though, because alongside the old writing desks nestled inside the elegant polished cabinets are row upon row of some of the world's finest photographic equipment, from the very latest technology to some of the very first cameras manufactured by Nikon. For me I suppose 'discover' is the wrong word; Grays of Westminster had always been there. I had seen their advertisements on the pages of popular photography magazines; I had even looked through their lists of equipment from time to time. But what use could a small shop over one hundred miles away in London be to me, an amateur photographer playing around with cameras in Bristol?

"A few years later I was making wildlife films for the BBC Natural History Unit and my 'playing with cameras' took on another dimension. We had played around with still images as back plates in the past and I once even used an oversized film back on an old F3. But it was when I was taking my first steps into the digital world that things really started to change and I realised I would need a very good supply of perfect Nikon lenses. After a limited search I naturally spoke to Grays and instantly started to realise how they had earned their unequalled reputation. From that very first conversation and subsequent visits, Grays of Westminster with its outstanding professionalism has not only become my main supplier of new and used equipment but they are also my advisors - from an old-style 20mm lens for a camera to be left on the Serengeti Plains filming migrating wildebeest to a modern 12-24mm lens to be stripped down to fit an underwater housing ready to film starfish under the thick sea ice of Antarctica.

"Throughout my adventures Gray and his team have always been there to support and advise me from the beginning ... even if it's to look at me in total disbelief at what I wanted to do next! So what can that small shop over one hundred miles away in London do for me? Well, anything and everything photographic, from the finest Nikon equipment to many fine words of wisdom. But the best thing still is that this small shop, which may appear to be locked away in time, with a past celebrated in the photographic museum that's down its narrow winding staircase, most definitely has its eye on the future.

"Over the years I've been lucky enough to work with and alongside some of the world's best and most renowned photographers: Jim Brandenburg, David Doubilet, Daniel Beltrá and Vincent Munier; recently when we were all together in London I made sure that a visit to Grays of Westminster was most definitely on our to-do list. And as a final comment, I'm often asked by friends both professional and amateur where to get certain 'bits of kit'. I always tell them to contact Grays of Westminster first, and so far none of them has ever been disappointed."

– Neil Lucas

CHAPTER 11
EXCLUSIVELY... NIKON

When Gray Levett decided that the company should specialize exclusively in Nikon in 1992, Nikon had already created a system that seemed as if it might defy obsolescence.

A rare Nikkor F camera made for the German market

Since 1959, and in particular with the introduction of the all-conquering Nikon F 35mm single lens reflex, Nikon had become the overwhelming choice for those who took photography seriously. Their market increased further when they announced the replacement of the king of professional 35mm SLR cameras in 1971 with a new flagship model, the Nikon F2.

Many professional and keen amateurs could not understand why the Nikon F could not just continue, with perhaps the odd improvement here and there. However, within a relatively short space of time, the F2 had established itself as not only a worthy successor to the title of the best Nikon SLR but also as a unique and worthy camera in its own right. The F2 was more than a simple improvement to the legendary Nikon F; it was the foundation of the entire Nikon system of 35mm photography and the world's largest 35mm system of lenses, accessories and motor drives. After building on the expanding Nikon F system, within a relatively short space of time, there were more than fifty-five Nikkor lenses available from a 6mm to a 2000mm, as well as a vast array of accessories.

1980 saw the release of the next flagship model, the mighty Nikon F3. The F3 was born into the tradition of rugged dependability and inherited the most comprehensive group of lenses and accessories ever assembled. Alongside the Nikon F selected by NASA, the United States National Aeronautics and Space Administration, for use in the Space Shuttle Program, a special version of the F3, modified to meet the unique environmental conditions encountered in space flight was subsequently selected as well. The Space Shuttle Program was the most ambitious technological venture of all time.

> “BY THE TIME GRAYS OF WESTMINSTER OPENED ITS SHOP PREMISES IN PIMLICO, NIKON AS A BRAND WAS FAST BECOMING THE LEADING ONE IN TECHNOLOGY, DESIGN AND RELIABILITY.

Nikon announced the replacement to the F3, the new Nikon F4 in 1988. The F4 was a professional model, which had, as one had come to expect from Nikon, interchangeable viewfinders and focusing screens, a mirror lock-up, a very fast motor drive and a 100% viewfinder. The F4 was designed to ensure that it would withstand extremes of temperature, vibration, humidity, bright light and heavy use. The F4 could take any Nikkor lens ever made, manual or autofocus.

By the time Grays of Westminster opened its shop premises in Pimlico, Nikon as a brand was fast becoming the leading one in technology, design and reliability.

Although Gray Levett had not yet consciously decided to go ‘exclusively Nikon’, he chose very early on not to stock compact and video cameras, nor to sell rolls of film or provide processing as a service. Instead, the decision was made to reserve the company’s efforts to making sure that each customer’s exact requirements and specifications for equipment were met, from locating perhaps a unique piece of equipment for a client that could not be found elsewhere to ensuring that a camera could be fast-tracked, if needed, to the far reaches of the world for an important shoot.

From 1989 onwards, although Grays of Westminster were without doubt successfully selling the full range of the top camera brands, Nikon, Canon, Minolta, Pentax, Leica, medium-format Hasselblad, Mamiya and Bronica, by 1992 Gray felt that some matters should be resolved with regard to the future.

His intention was always to move towards an ideal scene for his customers and to provide an outlet where both needs and service were equally tailored and inclusive. Many photographers at the time found it hard to easily obtain replacements for the odd little accessories – an eyepiece correction lens, any one of nine different dioptres, an obscure lens hood, a soft-focus filter. It seemed that, whereas the majority of camera dealers stocked major items such as camera bodies, lenses or flashguns, they did not usually keep the full range of the smaller specialist items in stock.

Gray concluded that providing the difficult-to-obtain items such as the correct lens hood,

Nikon
F3
high-eyepoint
Nikon
F3 LAPITA 2000
MEMORIAL EDITION
HP
BLACK
Made in Japan
Nikon

Grays of Westminster
Exclusively...Nikon
Nikon

the correct filter, the correct case, and having them readily available, would enormously benefit the photographer. He also began to look at the ramifications and the benefits of moving into a more focused market in order to encompass a wider range of equipment and yet specialise at the same time.

Against the background of the uneasiness surrounding the Gulf War between 1990 and 1991, a looming recession, high interest rates, rising unemployment and a sharp fall in demand for all types of housing began to affect many of the consumer markets.

It seemed that within the photographic trade, the mood was apprehensive and there were many dealers offering the same type of equipment as Grays of Westminster. Gray considered that a change of course might well avoid the company getting caught up in the decline and financial loss that was decimating many of the businesses at the time.

The solution came from an improbable area. On a very hot day in July 1991, Gray was walking through London's newly renovated Docklands, seeking shelter from the heat. He ducked into one of the many large warehouses converted to restaurants for a chilled beer and spotted a shop called The Christmas Shop which, even in the heatwave, was packed with customers buying Christmas tree trinkets. In spite of its unlikely merchandise for the time of the year, this highly specialist enterprise had somehow caught the imagination of a market in recession and was flourishing.

"I began to think that if you could run a successful business selling products that are only in use for about three weeks of the year, would it not be possible for Grays of Westminster to offer a specialist service just selling one brand and be equally successful?"

For many years, Gray had admired Nikon for their superb engineering and quality of their lenses. After some thoughtful analysis, he concluded that the periods which had been particularly successful over the previous few years were coincident with the times they had dealt more with Nikon equipment than any other brand. Furthermore, to his knowledge, at that time there was not another exclusively Nikon outlet anywhere in the world. If they went ahead, it would mean that Grays of Westminster would be re-created as a specialist outlet for Nikon enthusiasts and professionals alike. It would be a business that would sell contemporary Nikon bodies, lenses, and accessories, an exclusive purveyor for the collector of vintage Nikon, and a focal point for Nikon users everywhere. It would also mean that the photographer could purchase absolutely everything he or she needed in the way of Nikon equipment from one source.

Gray approached Nikon U.K. Limited, who agreed with the idea in principle; in order to become a 'Category A Dealer', Grays of Westminster were given a specific target to achieve within a year. Grays of Westminster reached that target in just over three months and were assigned the authorised dealership, Category A, on March 3rd 1992.

When Grays of Westminster became Grays of Westminster exclusively...Nikon, the logo simultaneously changed and was repeated throughout all the designs for the shop, from the letterhead to the elegant Oxford blue and gold carrier bags. The decision was to announce the change formally, almost as a proclamation, and the most manifestly visual way of doing so was in the creation of a distinctive flag.

A flag defines and represents the image of a nation, but it can also be a statement, the bearer of tidings, the emblem raised as a symbol to herald a new future.

It was Black & Edgington, the Royal flag makers, to whom Grays of Westminster entrusted the work. They had a long history dating back to the middle of the eighteenth century. For two hundred years their flags had graced numerous state and royal occasions, and they were privileged to hold the Royal Warrant from Her Majesty Queen Elizabeth II for the manufacture of flags and tents. At the opening of the Great Exhibition in 1851, it was Black & Edgington who had supplied all the British and foreign flags that flew above the Crystal Palace.

Black & Edgington's designs for the Grays of Westminster flag (which measures six feet by three feet) were approved and within a short space of time it was manufactured and installed in the balcony above the shop. As a person walks down Churton Street today, he can see the flag flying with the familiar Grays of Westminster...exclusively Nikon script set in gold against an Oxford blue background.

In 1992, regally standing for the first time over the shop from the balcony of the first floor, it bore the tidings of a new future... an exclusively Nikon future.

Whether enthusiast or professional, photographers have a professional result as their personal target. Being exclusively Nikon meant that when Nikon users, enthusiasts and professionals alike, became clients of Grays, they were able to focus their energies with an uncompromisingly professional approach on the equipment at hand. The most comprehensive camera system in the world can pose a rich variety of queries, which can arise whether the equipment is modern or vintage. Becoming exclusively Nikon meant that the staff at Grays of Westminster were able to fully take on their customers' questions and needs, undistracted by other matters. They could devote their energies and attention to Nikon: they worked with Nikon, they thought Nikon, and they understood Nikon.

It was new territory, yet within months of re-forming the company into an exclusively Nikon enterprise, they had somehow fashioned a camera shop packed with devotees and buzzing with enthusiastic clients as well as a business that was soon flourishing beyond expectation. ■

> "I BEGAN TO THINK ... WOULD IT NOT BE POSSIBLE FOR GRAYS OF WESTMINSTER TO OFFER A SPECIALIST SERVICE JUST SELLING ONE BRAND AND BE EQUALLY SUCCESSFUL?"

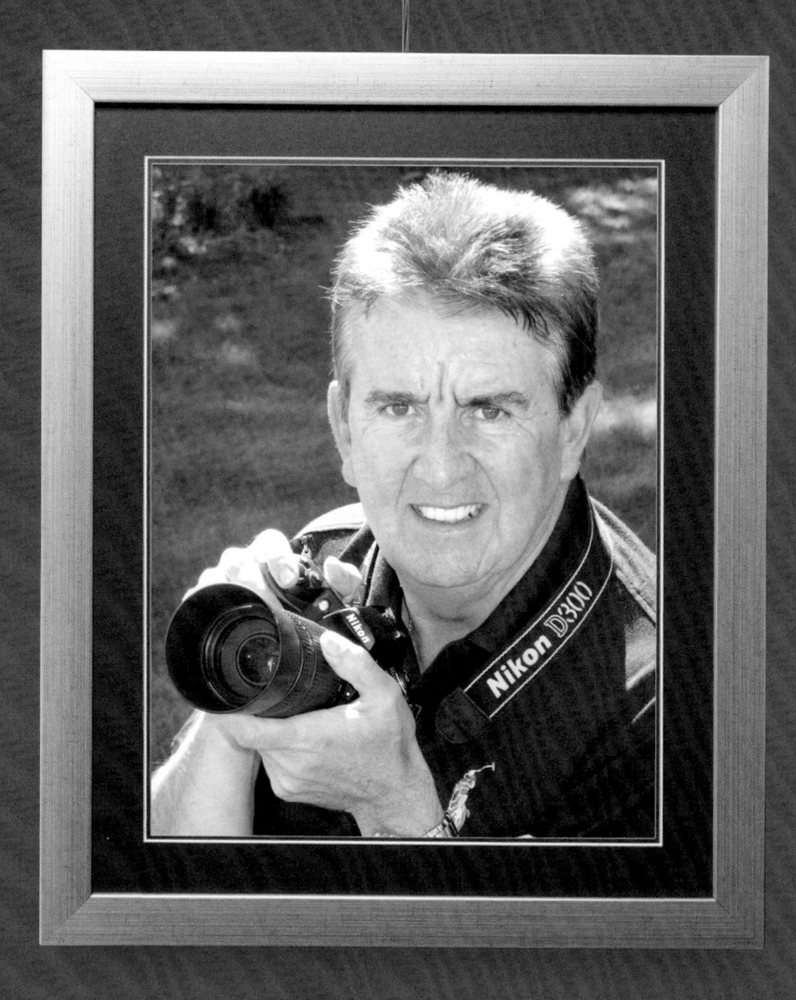

Prof. MIKE MALONEY, OBE

Mike Maloney is Britain's most decorated press photographer. During a career spanning more than 30 years, Dr. Mike Maloney OBE has won 107 major photographic honours, including being voted Press Photographer of the Year three times.

Mike was chief photographer for Mirror Group Newspapers before turning freelance in 2002. His work has taken him across the globe and introduced him to some of the world's most famous faces, including stars of stage and screen like Frank Sinatra, Mae West and Grace Kelly. He has photographed many world leaders including Clinton, Reagan, Gorbachev and Yeltsin, resulting in invitations to dine at the White House and the Kremlin.

He is perhaps best known for his work photographing the Royal Family, and was said to be the Queen Mother's favourite press photographer. He is the only Fleet Street photo-journalist to be awarded an OBE, receiving the honour in 2005. A Freeman of the City of London, he was also awarded an Honorary Doctorate of Arts by the University of Lincoln in 2001. It is believed he is the first Fleet Street photographer to be awarded a Professorship of Photography.

"People I talk to in the photographic business always sing the praises of Grays of Westminster.

"If you want a Nikon shopping experience there is no finer place to go. Phrases like 'so professional to deal with' and 'top quality used gear – really looks like new' you hear time and time again. I am a great believer in word-of-mouth advertising and I have never heard a single person say anything uncomplimentary about Grays of Westminster. For someone who works in the photographic industry I find that most unusual.

"Grays of Westminster is masterminded by a gentleman called Gray Levett – one of the most honourable, knowledgeable and pleasant men you could ever wish to meet. Many years ago, before I had had the pleasure of meeting Mr. Levett, my editor at Amateur Photographer magazine suggested that I go out of my way to visit his emporium in London`s Pimlico district. 'You two will get on really well.' How right he was. Entering the magnificent quintessential Nikon dealership reminded me of Doctor Who`s TARDIS – not very large on the outside but step into the beautifully furnished interior and it is huge! It is not often that one encounters so many beautifully presented pieces of camera equipment – a Nikon Aladdin`s Cave.

"It is the only camera shop I have ever visited where you will find a boxed, mint condition 1950`s Nikon F SLR alongside the very latest digital Nikon D810. Furthermore the staff are so knowledgeable, courteous and inspirational. I have always said that:

"The mediocre camera shop tells.
"The good camera shop explains.
"The superior camera shop demonstrates.
"The great camera shop . . . inspires!

"I would like to take this opportunity to congratulate Grays of Westminster on their 30-year anniversary and raise a glass to their next thirty. As my old Latin teacher at school in Lincoln would have said about Grays of Westminster: 'Cygnus inter anates – a swan amongst ducks.'"

– Prof. Mike Maloney, OBE

CHAPTER 12
AN AMERICAN IN LONDON

With the ongoing digital revolution, Nikon's own interpretation of the needs of their public and their consequent new developments have consistently captured the marketplace with their range of new DSLRs and Nikkor lenses.

Through a thoughtful and intelligent utilisation of new technology, combined with their usual unparalleled workmanship, they have caught the interest of the professional and enthusiast photographer alike, and advancement and development is such that new major releases in Nikon products have occurred more frequently than in earlier years.

Grays of Westminster strive to put in as much thought to presenting and selling the product as Nikon do with its development and production. It was always important to Gray Levett to seek out very able individuals as directors and members of staff so that he could have the finest, most knowledgeable team at Grays to assist the vast range of customers with their varying needs and requirements.

Now one of the directors and a co-partner of Grays of Westminster with Gray Levett, Uri Zakay joined the sales department at Grays of Westminster in November 1998. Although Grays of Westminster already had far-reaching contacts all over the world, with a mix of enthusiastic vitality and agile business acumen, Uri helped to create a new level of expansion within the company, working with

Gray Levett to make Grays of Westminster even more accessible to an entirely new, world-wide photographic public.

almost as a natural progression from this, the subject of economics and the art of business began to appeal to me as well."

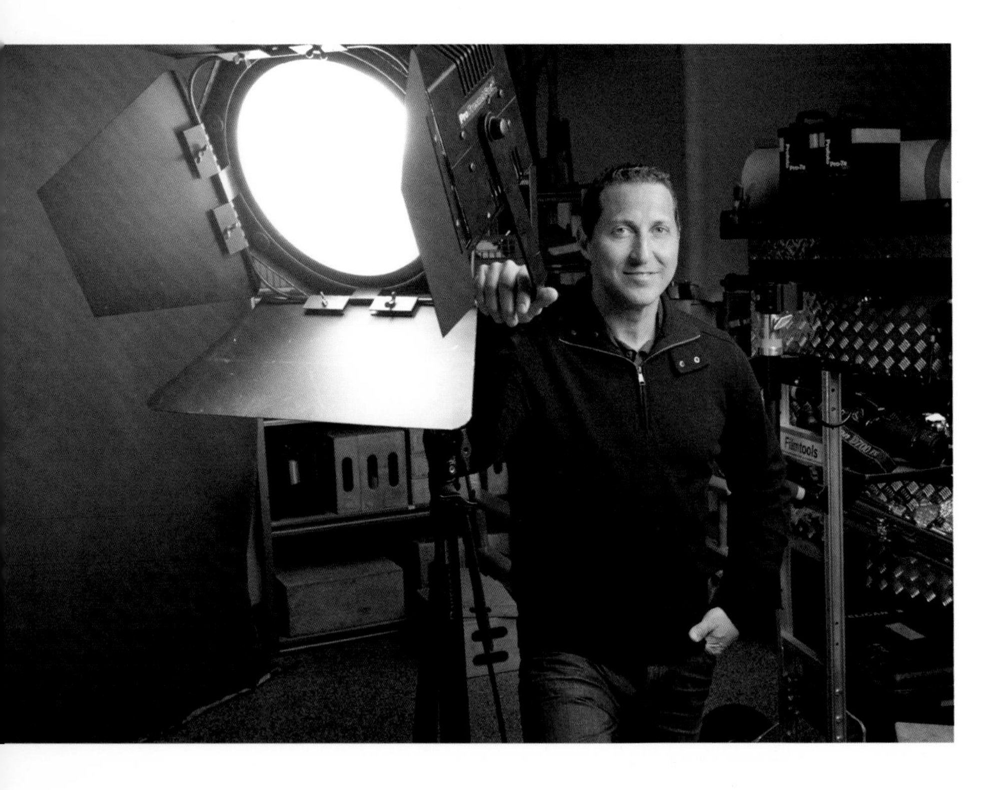

Like Gray, he categorically believes in providing the ultimate service for the client and says that it was always a personal dream to create or work within the perfect retail business that would give the customer everything they came for and much more.

Uri was born in Tel Aviv in 1971 and moved to Los Angeles with his family ten years later. With a father who was a lecturer at Tel Aviv University and a mother who always had an unwavering belief in human rights and a desire to help people improve their lives, Uri grew up in a home which had strong moral values. He said however, that the move from Israel to Los Angeles at the age of ten was initially something of a surprise.

"In the beginning, it was a bit of a shock to the system, but very quickly I learned to love the freedoms of the U.S.A., the outdoor life and in particular the emphasis on sport. In fact, being very involved in football and athletics at school enabled me to adjust to the American lifestyle really fast. I was very competitive as a young teenager and wanted to achieve a high standard in whatever I did. Sport helped me do that. As I moved through my teens and early twenties,

He observed that while working at any company if you try to provide the best service you possibly can and you are loyal to your customers, they tend to be loyal to you. Likewise, if you provide a less than helpful service, or a service that only consists of the bare basics, your clientele might well look elsewhere.

"I have been involved in other businesses in the past and attempted to achieve the goal of providing the best service possible for the customer without much success, mainly because the other people working with me did not deem it necessary. Gray Levett at Grays of Westminster shared with me the belief that people were important and that it was far better to give customers more than they ever expected or asked for."

With a base both in Los Angeles and London, Uri is also able to maintain the contacts originally made by Gray Levett during his earlier period in Hollywood. ■

> GRAY LEVETT AT GRAYS OF WESTMINSTER SHARED WITH ME THE BELIEF THAT PEOPLE WERE IMPORTANT AND THAT IT WAS FAR BETTER TO GIVE CUSTOMERS MORE THAN THEY EVER EXPECTED OR ASKED FOR.

SIR SIMON MARSDEN

Sir Simon Marsden (1 December 1948 – 22 January 2012) was an internationally acclaimed photographer of the fantastic and the supernatural who devoted his life to photographing ancient ruins and landscapes, capturing in his images the atmosphere of their mysterious past and the eerie presence of the spirits that are still believed to haunt them. His images can be found in many prestigious collections, including the Getty Museum in California, the Victoria & Albert Museum in London and the Bibliothèque Nationale in Paris. He also exhibited in New York, London, Brussels, Milan and Tokyo.

His books include Russia: *A World Apart, The Haunted Realm - Echoes from Beyond the Tomb, In Ruins - The Once Great Houses of Ireland, Phantoms of the Isles - Further Tales from The Haunted Realm, Visions of Poe - A Personal Selection of Edgar Allan Poe's Stories and Poems, The Journal of a Ghosthunter - In Search of the Undead from Ireland to Transylvania, Beyond the Wall - The Lost World of East Germany, Venice - City of Haunting Dreams, The Twilight Hour - Celtic Visions from the Past, This Spectred Isle - A Journey Through Haunted England, Ghosthunter - A Journey through Haunted France, Memento Mori - Churches* and *Churchyards of England and Vampires: The Twilight World.*

"As a fine art photographer who has spent a lifetime printing his own photographs I am more interested in putting something of myself into the end print, than in the technicalities of the equipment I use. Because of the strength of this creative urge my knowledge of cameras is often wanting and I have always been wary of visiting a photographic store. Too often the staff bombard you with a plethora of unintelligible information, with only one thing in mind - to make a quick sale, and forget you just as soon as you are out of the door.

"I discovered Grays of Westminster in 1992 and remember feeling instantly at ease as I wandered downstairs, marvelling at the collection of old and new Nikons in the large glass cabinets. After a while a gentleman came in and sat at a desk. We both smiled at each other and carried on with what we were doing. Eventually he asked me if he could help, and two hours later I found myself on my third cup of coffee discussing various experiences we had both had of the paranormal. To my great relief I had met Gray Levett the owner, a like spirit, who has since supported my work in many ways and sympathetically filled in the technical gaps in my photographic knowledge.

"Those of us who have spent hours, days, sometimes weeks in a darkroom at a time are now a dying breed with the rapid advance of digital photography. It has always been difficult to return to the real world after spending so much time fantasising in this small, darkened room – rather like being cut off in the tower of a great gothic castle with only one's imagination and the chemical magic as one's friends. Gray, knowledgeable in both the new and the old forms of photography, like the alchemists of the past recognises that the marriage of opposites, in their case the mystery of nature and the reality of science, is the way forward. He is therefore invaluable to a photographer like myself as a guide through this rapidly changing medium and his shop a peaceful haven from the stress and madness of our modern day world."

– Sir Simon Marsden

CHAPTER 13
AT YOUR SERVICE
THE STAFF AT GRAYS OF WESTMINSTER

Behind Grays of Westminster's renowned reputation is the team that looks after the customers in the shop or on the telephone, as well as a whole group of dedicated staff working hard behind the scenes.

Gray said, *"As the founder of Grays of Westminster, there have been many constants in my life. The team at Grays of Westminster has played a major part throughout and without each of them, together and individually, I would not have been able to create the company we have today. Our staff are a key factor to our success because I have always held as sacred that our customers deserve the very best in staff and service."*

Many of the team have been working at Grays of Westminster for a very long time indeed. Five, ten, fifteen years is the norm rather than the exception.

Although there are many different departments with a wide variety of duties within the structure at Grays of Westminster: the sales team, the technical team, the editorial team and the administrative team, they all hold in common the ideal of providing an exemplary level of service for the customer whether he or she visits the shop or phones in with an order. The personnel who take on many of the supporting roles also play a very significant part in the smooth running of the company.

I asked some of the staff about their experience of working at Grays of Westminster.

TABITHA HARDY, the sales manager, who started working at Grays in 1994, told me, *"It is always a pleasure to look after our customers and it is important to me as the sales manager that the whole sales team are prepared to go the extra mile to ensure our customers are well looked after. We have many regular clients that feel like family, and I love to hear about their photographic adventures. In fact, it isn't like any other business I have worked in before."*

BECKY DANESE, one of the main technical advisors, has been working at Grays of Westminster since 2008. She said, *"The team at Grays is like an extended family; everyone has something different to offer but we all hold the same values in mind: that our customers, no matter who they are, are important. I personally try to ensure that every person taking home a Nikon camera or lens knows how to use it, how to get the best out of it and how to forward their photography with their new purchase. I am on hand to assist with solutions whether it be simple settings or a larger conundrum."*

KONSTANTIN KOCHKIN, like Becky Danese, a senior technical advisor, provides technical support to the customers over the phone and in person; he has been working at Grays since 2008. *"My job is making sure that a customer's needs are fully understood and the best solution for that individual customer is always my main priority. I also feel that I am blessed working with such wonderful and passionate group of people such as the Grays of Westminster team."*

CAROLINE NOLAN joined Grays of Westminster in 2007; she works on special projects for the directors. *"I enjoy working as part of a team that offers such a great service to Nikon users and I am proud that so many of our customers return time and time again. As far as the Grays of Westminster team is concerned, you'd be hard pushed to find a friendlier and more caring group of people to work alongside."*

RAFFI SILVANIAN, senior sales assistant since 2010, agreed, *"I think customer care is vitally important and we all aim to courteously assist the customer find the product most suitable to his needs and to understand and answer his questions. I take great pleasure in working at Grays of Westminster because of the professionalism and high standards of the directors and the rest of the team. It is also a very pleasant working environment, and I thoroughly enjoy any of the challenges that might come my way"*.

MARK GIBSON, Director of Photography, has been working with Grays of Westminster since 2007. He told me: *"Using Nikon DSLRs, I have produced various corporate films that have had nearly half a million views including the Grays of Westminster DVD. Having run my own business in the past in Savile Row providing a bespoke service, I am fully aware of the importance of exemplary service."*

Grays of Westminster

25th Anniversary 1985 – 2011

Grays of Westminster, the multi-award-winning Nikon-only shop was founded in 1985 by Gray Levett with the idea of creating a world-class camera store, offering a service that was second to none. Thus the germ of an idea began to take shape which would eventually come to life as Grays of Westminster.

"Grays of Westminster is a well-known and respected business that has become almost a household name amongst professional photographers during the last twenty-five years. This is no doubt the result of your commitment to your customers and understanding of the Nikon brand."
– Makoto Kimura, President
Nikon Corporation, Japan

"Grays of Westminster – The High Church of Nikon."
– Professional Photographer magazine

"Grays of Westminster – The kind of service of which legends are made."
– Amateur Photographer magazine

"Grays of Westminster – A true retailing phenomenon."
– BPI – British Photographic Industry News

KATRIN RUCKERT began working at Grays of Westminster in 2009 as an administrator. She currently coordinates the various events, workshops, safaris and photo-tours that are organized. She said, *"Having been an active photographer myself, I really enjoy dealing with both photographic enthusiasts and professional photographers alike and sharing the results of their endeavours. The team here at Grays is friendly, professional, and simply very enjoyable to work with, more than any other place I have worked in the past."*

PABLO MONTEAGUDO joined the sales team of Grays of Westminster in 2013; he is multi-lingual and is able to deal with the ever-increasing number of customers from abroad. *"As a keen enthusiast, I always try to put myself in the position of the customer; I provide for each person as much information for choice as I possibly can, using practical examples, trying to help them make the most informed decisions. Grays of Westminster is an inspiring place, with a multi-cultural team that keeps you learning and finding new ways of thinking all the time."*

TRACEY WINSKILL, the shipping manager for Grays of Westminster has worked for Grays of Westminster for more than thirteen years. It is Tracey and her team that take pride in ensuring that any lens, body or accessory reaches its destination with the minimum of fuss, packaged expertly and within record time. *"It doesn't matter where in the world you need your package or how complex the delivery instructions are, we make a plan! As for working with the Grays' team, although we are very focused on customer care, we do also make sure we look after each other."*

ENIKO VARADI has been working for Grays of Westminster since 2013, as a senior administrative assistant for both *Nikon Owner* and Grays of Westminster. She deals with the administration of subscriptions and says, *"I enjoy working at Grays of Westminster because I feel the environment and team dynamic created within the business is a wonderful one to work in, and the effort I put into my work is always really appreciated."*

DANIEL CROFT, who works in the sales department, enjoys working at Grays because *"We have a great group of friendly, knowledgeable staff, who are very professional, while not taking themselves too seriously."* He ensures that all the questions a customer might have are fully answered, and that they are provided with the equipment they need, in order to get the results they want to achieve. He has been working at Grays of Westminster since 2011.

ANDREJA OBADIC started working for Grays of Westminster in 2014 as an administrative assistant. *"I strive to provide excellent customer service through entering data into the mailing system to help both the sales team and the clients. I enjoy working for Grays of Westminster; there is always a nice atmosphere in the shop and great team spirit between the staff. I'm one of the newest member of the team and have been accepted at face value with lots of help from everyone."*

Of particular note are two key former members of staff who worked for Grays of Westminster for a number of years until they retired. Toni Kowal, who spoke fluent Japanese and had a post-graduate degree in applied optics, was very knowledgeable in the vintage camera field, and travelled to Japan regularly (over 200 visits in total) as the senior buyer for Grays of Westminster to source exceptionally rare or significant Nikon items. Bron Kowal, his brother, was multi-lingual and had gained his expertise in the photographic industry at Vintage Cameras Ltd., as well as having had extensive experience in publishing. He was a member of the senior sales-team.

Gray Levett explains what is different about Grays of Westminster:

"When our clients go out of the door, whether they have purchased a lens hood or the latest camera, this is not the end of it – we hope to have a long-running relationship with each of them. We deliberately set out not simply to sell equipment. Although this is very important and very necessary, we also want to offer an old-fashioned and friendly service in a modern age.

"It has always been my belief that it is far, far better to give people more than they feel they should expect. For example, this may amount to a better part-exchange price on their old equipment, or providing them with a minutely-detailed answer to a question raised in an email, phone call or personal visit.

"It may mean that the combination of extra warranties we offer on new equipment, those extra discounts and personal attention to detail unmatched in the photographic industry comes to bear on each and every individual that we look after. Then again a friendly welcome and a deep belief in giving that person exactly what he wants and letting him know that the questions he raises and the photographic queries he has are important. Everyone is important and there are no exceptions."

"MY GOAL HAS ALWAYS BEEN TO CREATE A SHOP THAT IS AN ELEGANT OASIS OF OLD-FASHIONED SERVICE. IT IS MY UNSTINTING DETERMINATION TO RELATE TO OUR CUSTOMERS WITH THE SPIRIT, COURTESY AND ENTHUSIASM NOW SO OFTEN LOST TO THE MODERN RETAIL WORLD...

For many retail businesses, once a transaction is completed and the salesman has made his quota of sales, the customer is forgotten, whereas for the team at Grays of Westminster, the sale is often only the beginning of the relationship. Nikon users, like many other members of the purchasing public today, frequently scan the internet for 'the best deal'. It takes shrewd business decisions for any company to maintain its place in such a variable price market. But most importantly, the directors and staff are committed to working together to ensure that Grays of Westminster aims to give the customer a service second to none.

Gray Levett says, *"My goal has always been to create a shop that is an elegant oasis of old-fashioned service. It is my unstinting determination to relate to our customers with the spirit, courtesy and enthusiasm now so often lost to the modern retail world, to attend to detail because it practically matters, to inform and advise because we can and to afford to each and every one of our customers the same grace, willingness and good manners that we believe everyone is due."* ■

JOE McNALLY

Joe McNally is an internationally acclaimed photographer whose career has spanned more than 30 years and has included assignments in 60 countries. Over the years he has been an ongoing contributor to *National Geographic*, a contract photographer for *Sports Illustrated* and shot numerous cover stories for *TIME*, *Newsweek*, *Fortune*, *New York* and *The New York Times Sunday Magazine*. McNally regularly writes a popular blog about the travails, tribulations and high moments of being a photographer and has authored several books on photography. He was recently named as one of the 'Top Five Most Socially Influential Photographers', and 'The 2015 Photographer of the Year'. He has bridged the world between photojournalism and advertising, with a client list that includes FedEx, Nikon, Epson, Sony, General Electric, MetLife, USAA, Adidas, ESPN, the Beijing Cultural Commission and American Ballet Theater. As a workshop instructor and lecturer, he has taught at a number of institutions including the National Geographic Society, Smithsonian Institution, the Disney Institute, and the U.S.A. Department of Defense. He is a Nikon U.S.A. Ambassador, an honour that has a special significance for him, as he bought his first Nikon camera in 1973, and for forty years, from the deserts of Africa to the snows of Siberia, he has seen the world through those cameras. He received his bachelor's and graduate degrees from Syracuse University's S.I. Newhouse School of Public Communications.
http://portfolio.joemcnally.com

USAA United Services Automobile Association
ESPN Entertainment & Sports Programming Network

"London is a grand city of legend and lore, and it can be understood that when one speaks of the important jewels of this city, one is referencing the glittering treasures known as the Crown Jewels. Housed in the Tower of London, those glittering, precious stones draw millions of visitors yearly, and are justly spoken of as one of the historically important wonders of the globe.

"However, London is also a city made up of smaller jewels, not in the news as much, perhaps, and requiring no tickets or tours. They are simply there for the finding. One such jewel is that legendary cache of Nikon cameras and lenses known as Grays of Westminster. Its reputation for service and stock has won this stunning emporium of Nikon gear literally every award imaginable in the photo world, and it is the first-ever camera store to be awarded the legendary Coat of Arms.

"Given the fact that Nikon cameras and lenses are themselves the stuff of legend, this is not surprising. While in the store, time is wonderfully warped, and when there I find myself not wanting to leave. You can walk in and fully outfit yourself as a modern, digital age photographer, and at the same time, wander leisurely through Nikon history, viewing iconic Nikon F's and never to be made again lenses.

"There are lenses and cameras in these glass cases that are wonderful pieces of my photographic memory, such as the high speed F2H camera bodies I used for space shuttle launches, and rare fisheyes I have suspended beneath helicopters. It reminds you of the durability and usability of these redoubtable pieces of equipment you once pounded in the field as a photographer on a daunting location shoot, and here they are again, polished, under glass – like the crown jewels.

"Grays of Westminster rightly claims a place in Nikon's history, and in the history of camera stores the world over. It is a perennial stop for me when in London. The gracious welcome extended to everyone, the sense of service, even the very scale and architecture of the place speaks of an era gone by, yet at the same time, somehow, remains resolutely current. The creator of this amazing place, Gray Levett, has done an extraordinary thing – he has woven together technology, history, depth of knowledge and attention to detail into a place that certainly cannot be referred to as a 'camera shop.' It is a memorable experience every Nikon shooter should have."

–Joe McNally

CHAPTER 14
THE GRAYS OF WESTMINSTER GAZETTE & THE FOUNDING OF NIKON OWNER MAGAZINE

The word 'magazine' ultimately derives from the Arabic makhazin (storehouses) by way of the French language. The term was initially used by *The Gentleman's Magazine*, published in 1731 in London and considered to have been the first general-interest magazine.

The editor was Edward Cave, using the pen name of 'Sylvanus Urban'. Since that time, magazines of all topics and disciplines have thrived, providing both inspiration and a relaxed form of imparting knowledge or information to their readers.

The *Grays of Westminster Gazette* was launched in August 1992. It was created to keep the Nikon user close to the hub of Nikon development and products, accessories and latest techniques as well as fully informed on the continuing evolution of the Nikon system.

Initially four pages long, then eight, now thirty-six, it contains a wide range of intelligent articles and images on the latest Nikon equipment, and is sent out to Grays of Westminster's 49,000 customers.

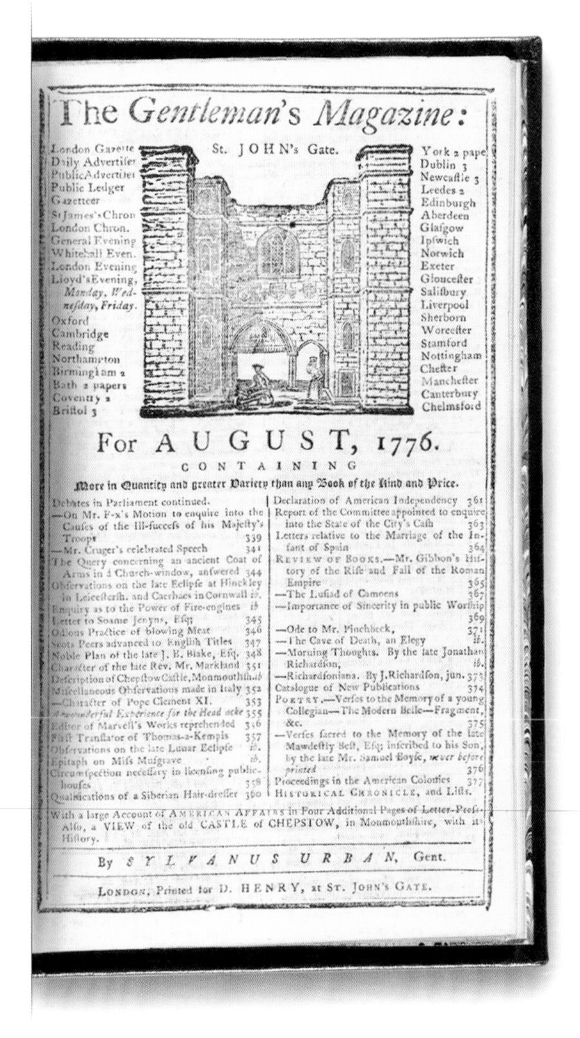

The *Gentleman's Magazine*:

London Gazette
Daily Advertiser
Public Advertiser
Public Ledger
Gazetteer
St James's Chron
London Chron.
General Evening
Whitehall Even.
London Evening
Lloyd's Evening, *Monday, Wednesday, Friday.*
Oxford
Cambridge
Reading
Northampton
Birmingham 2
Bath 2 papers
Coventry 2
Bristol 3

St. JOHN's Gate.

York 2 pape
Dublin 3
Newcastle 3
Leedes 2
Edinburgh
Aberdeen
Glasgow
Ipswich
Norwich
Exeter
Gloucester
Salisbury
Liverpool
Sherborn
Worcester
Stamford
Nottingham
Chester
Manchester
Canterbury
Chelmsford

For AUGUST, 1776.

CONTAINING

More in Quantity and greater Variety than any Book of the Kind and Price.

Debates in Parliament continued.
—On Mr. F-x's Motion to enquire into the Causes of the ill-success of his Majesty's Troops 339
—Mr. Cruger's celebrated Speech 341
The Query concerning an ancient Coat of Arms in a Church-window, answered 344
Observations on the late Eclipse at Hinckley in Leicestersh. and Caerhaes in Cornwall ib.
Enquiry as to the Power of Fire-engines ib
Letter to Soame Jenyns, Esq; 345
Odious Practice of blowing Meat 346
Scots Peers advanced to English Titles 347
Noble Plan of the late J. B. Blake, Esq. 348
Character of the late Rev. Mr. Markland 351
Description of Chepstow Castle, Monmouthsh. ib
Miscellaneous Observations made in Italy 352
—Character of Pope Clement XI. 353
A wonderful Experience for the Head ache 355
Editor of Marvell's Works reprehended 356
First Translator of Thomas-a-Kempis 357
Observations on the late Lunar Eclipse ib.
Epitaph on Miss Musgrave ib.
Circumspection necessary in licensing public-houses 358
Qualifications of a Siberian Hair-dresser 360
Declaration of American Independency 361
Report of the Committee appointed to enquire into the State of the City's Cash 363
Letters relative to the Marriage of the Infant of Spain 364
REVIEW OF BOOKS.—Mr. Gibbon's History of the Rise and Fall of the Roman Empire 365
—The Lusiad of Camoens 367
—Importance of Sincerity in public Worship 369
—Ode to Mr. Pinchbeck, 371
—The Cave of Death, an Elegy ib.
—Morning Thoughts. By the late Jonathan Richardson, ib.
—Richardsoniana. By J. Richardson, jun. 373
Catalogue of New Publications 374
POETRY.—Verses to the Memory of a young Collegian—The Modern Belle—Fragment, &c. 375
—Verses sacred to the Memory of the late Mawdestly Best, Esq; inscribed to his Son, by the late Mr. Samuel Boyse, *never before printed* 376
Proceedings in the American Colonies 377
HISTORICAL CHRONICLE, and Lists.

With a large Account of AMERICAN AFFAIRS in Four Additional Pages of Letter-Press. Also, a VIEW of the old CASTLE of CHEPSTOW, in Monmouthshire, with its History.

By *SYLVANUS URBAN*, Gent.

LONDON, Printed for D. HENRY, at ST. JOHN's GATE.

The Grays of Westminster Gazette
ISSUE No. 6 Oct/Nov 1993
The Periodical for the Nikon Devotee
ISSUE No. 7 Dec/Jan 1993/94
ISSUE No. 11 Sept/Oct 1994
ISSUE No. 17 June 1995
ISSUE No. 13 Jan/Feb 1995
ISSUE No. 14 March 1995
ISSUE No. 16 May 1995
ISSUE No. 15 April 1995
THE RIDDLE OF TH
AF-I TELECONVERTERS
GAZETTE
Grays of Westminster
Exclusively...Nikon
The Periodical for the Nikon Devotee Founded 1992 • Issue No. 67
Nikon D810 Overview
by Simon Stafford
and much more...
The Grays of Westminster Coat of Arms 'Lead in Order to Serve'
by Gillian Greenwood
Nikon Df – Photography for the Soul
By Becky Danese
NEWS
There have been a number of very exciting new products announced by the Nikon Corporation recently.
Zoom-Nikkor AF VR 80-400mm f4.5-5.6D ED

Many of the earlier *Grays of Westminster Gazettes* have become collectables.

The concept of *Nikon Owner* magazine was created by Gray Levett, Uri Zakay and myself over twelve years ago and I have been fortunate enough to have been the Senior Features Editor since its inception. It is a magazine for Nikon users whose interests might include a profusion of interests from wildlife, natural history, landscape, digital, film, infrared, portraiture, astro-photography, macro, architectural, action/adventure, concert/theatre, fashion, reportage and still life to sport, transport and underwater photography.

Nikon Owner has a comprehensive interactive website, which contains a technical helpline, equipment reviews, special articles and a website gallery where each member can display his own work. Many Nikon users have used it as a support system for their photography, others as a point of inspiration. Much consideration and time was spent assembling the editorial team. Gray Levett, with a lifetime of knowledge in all things Nikon, is the Editor of *Nikon Owner*.

Simon Stafford, one of the world's leading technical experts on Nikon, is the Senior Technical Editor. His work has been published widely in a multitude of newspapers, books, calendars and magazines. With over thirty years of using the Nikon system in both film and digital photography, he brings his considerable expertise to bear as senior technical editor of *Nikon Owner*.

Becky Danese is the Sub-Editor and technical writer; she joined the *Nikon Owner* team last year, having worked in the technical department at Grays of Westminster since 2008. An accomplished photographer herself, she has excellent knowledge in both the digital and film aspect of photography and has used Nikon for many years.

Jesse Wilson is the Designer & Art Director for *Nikon Owner* and is an accomplished and prolific designer, having designed over 400 album covers and over 250 websites for various firms and individuals including photographers Mike Maloney OBE and the late Sir Simon Marsden, Grays of Westminster and many others.

The formation of *Nikon Owner* was announced and the first issue of the magazine was worked on and published. There was an unprecedented response: the *Sunday Express* devoted a full-page to its front cover, a never-before published image of Princess Diana, taken by eminent celebrity photographer Richard Young.

From those first tentative footsteps *Nikon Owner* has grown to the point where it has subscribers all over the world, from Australia and New Zealand to Japan and the U.S.A.. The editorial and management teams are in contact with the subscribers regularly to invite their thoughts and comments.

As *Nikon Owner* magazine is devoted entirely to Nikon equipment and Nikon users, it strives to keep its subscribers fully updated on all the latest developments in the Nikon world. A few years ago, Gray Levett, as editor of *Nikon Owner* and founder of Grays of Westminster, was given the opportunity, courtesy of an invitation from the President of Nikon Imaging, to have a private tour of the Sendai factory in northern Japan and to visit the Tokyo Headquarters of Nikon. He was personally briefed on the history of the factory, which was established in 1971. While he was there, he was not only given a full tour of the factory, but he was shown a pre-production sample of the particular digital SLR which had just started production. On the third day of his visit, he was invited for a meeting with the President of Nikon Imagining Division, Mr Michio Kariya. It was Mr Kariya, who as a young visionary engineer, had headed the team that developed ED (extra-low-dispersion) Nikkor Glass, the zenith of Nikon's achievements in optical design.

Over the years, *Nikon Owner* magazine has featured spectacular photography and in-depth articles by (or interviews with) some of the world's greatest photographers and photographic writers. These include Scott Andrews, Heather Angel, Tami Bahat, Sue Bishop, Jim Brandenburg, Michael Bright, Julian Calder, Michael Doven, David duChemin, Graham Eaton, Richard Edlund, Bruce Fleming, Graham Hancock & Santha Faiia, Paul Joynson-Hicks, Felix Kunze, Neil Lucas, Philip Makanna, Mike Maloney OBE, the late Sir Simon Marsden, Chris Martin, Patrick McMullan, Joe McNally, U.S. Nikon Ambassador Moose Peterson, Ken Regan, Martin Shann, Brian Slater, John Archer-Thomson, Mark Tillie, Simon Weir, Chris Weston, Andrew Main Wilson and Richard Young. Many of the unique interviews for *Nikon Owner* have been conducted by Michael Eleftheriades or Robert Falconer.

The celebrated actor David Suchet CBE has been featured twice in *Nikon Owner*. *Nikon Owner* has also published articles on Clint Eastwood, Denzel Washington, the late Stanley Kubrick and Frank Sinatra, all of whom have been Nikon users. Two of *Nikon Owner's* front covers have featured Her Majesty The Queen, taken by photographer Julian Calder.

The magazine covers the latest Nikon equipment reviews by Simon Stafford, as well as technique articles on an array of subjects. The Nikon historian has been catered for with articles on vintage Nikon by Gray Levett, illustrated in each issue by legendary photographer Tony Hurst. Articles or a series of articles by a number of *Nikon Owner* subscribers, including Matt Adams, Clive Carpenter, Phil and Tim Collier, Karen Hall, Anna Harbour, Michael Huggan, Steve Hughes, Will Nicholls, Robert Sanger, Esther Sonneveld Laveau and Guy Swarbrick can also be found.

Gray Levett states *"Nikon Owner has been enormously successful, and has taken off in an unprecedented way, which was completely unexpected."*

Over the last ten years not only has the magazine itself as a publication expanded in breadth and substance, but has provided its readers with a number of useful benefits, including group meetings and outings[6] for Nikon users throughout the U.K. and the opportunity to attend workshops, seminars, events, safaris and photographic tours, which cover a wide range of topics from Flash, Portraiture, Macro, Street Photography and other kit-related workshops to Lightroom, Panoramic and Colour-Calibration seminars. For a number of years, Grays of Westminster together with *Nikon Owner* also hosted successful wildlife and natural history photographic weekend workshops for *Nikon Owner* subscribers and Grays of Westminster customers at Saint Hill Manor, reputed to be the finest eighteenth-century sandstone manor house in Sussex with an interior design of some note; John Spencer Churchill, nephew of Sir Winston Churchill,

Heather Angel
OWNER
Nikon
NIKON OWNER GALLERY
Daniel Beltrá
ANGEL EYES XIV
by Heather Angel
Nippon Kogaku Japan
Nikon
Hurst Gallery • Technical
OWNER
Nikon
ISSUE XLVIII • 2014
ANDREW MAIN WILSON'S
EPIC ADVENTURE
ANGEL EYES XX
by Heather Angel
TAKEDOWN: THE DNA
OF GSP by Michael Bright
and Neil Lucas
Plus more...
OF LIGHT:
OWNER
Nikon
ISSUE XLIX
MAIN WILSON'S

Saint Hill Manor, Sussex

for example, painted the splendid mural for the 'Monkey Room' in the Manor in 1945. Saint Hill Manor itself has had a number of celebrated owners: Robert Crawfurd, who was instrumental in having the first railway to East Grinstead built in 1845, the Crookshank family from 1889 to 1945, The Maharajah of Jaipur, and more recently the humanitarian and award-winning photographer L. Ron Hubbard.

The workshops featured the world-renowned wildlife and natural history photographer, Heather Angel, with some attendees travelling from as far afield as New Zealand, Australia, India, U.S.A., Japan and South America as well as from all over the U.K. and Europe to participate. Grays of Westminster also hosted and organized several very successful and well-attended events with distinguished presenters such as Jo and Rob Gambi, who together hold the Guinness World Record for the fastest (and first) '7 Summits' ascent by a married couple (Jo holds the Guinness World Record for the fastest '7 Summits' ascent by a female), as well as presentations by the late Sir Simon Marsden and best-selling author Graham Hancock, whose books have sold more than five million copies worldwide. Graham's talk was illustrated by images by his wife, the eminent photographer Santha Faiia.

Another prestigious event on the calendar is the Christmas Event, held at the distinguished Institute of Directors, 116 Pall Mall, London. The eighteenth-century building is a landmark of London's great Georgian Heritage, owned by the Crown Estate and is Grade I listed. Guest speakers at this annual event have included such prestigious photographers as Scott Andrews, Jim Brandenburg, Julian Calder, Neil Lucas, Mike Maloney OBE, Andrew Main Wilson and Richard Young.

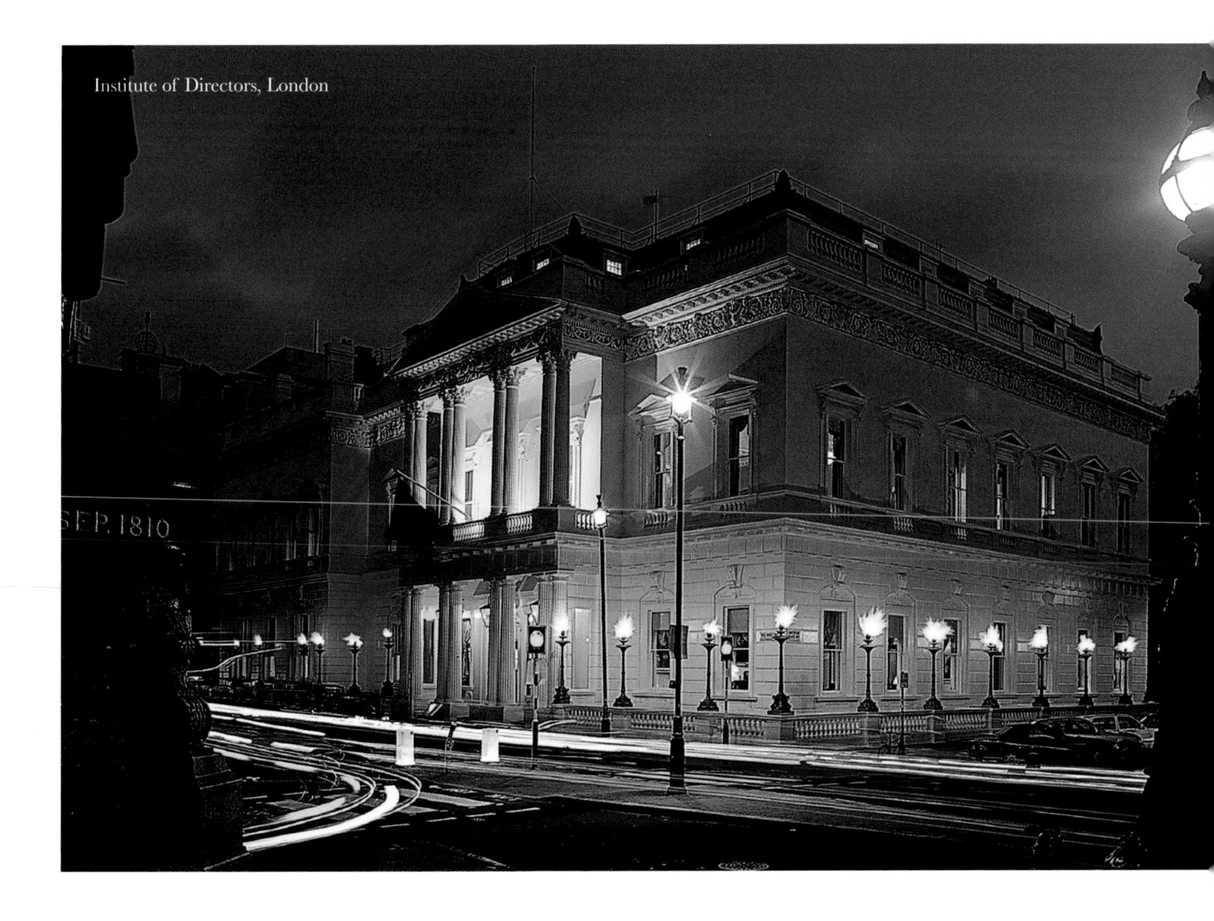

Institute of Directors, London

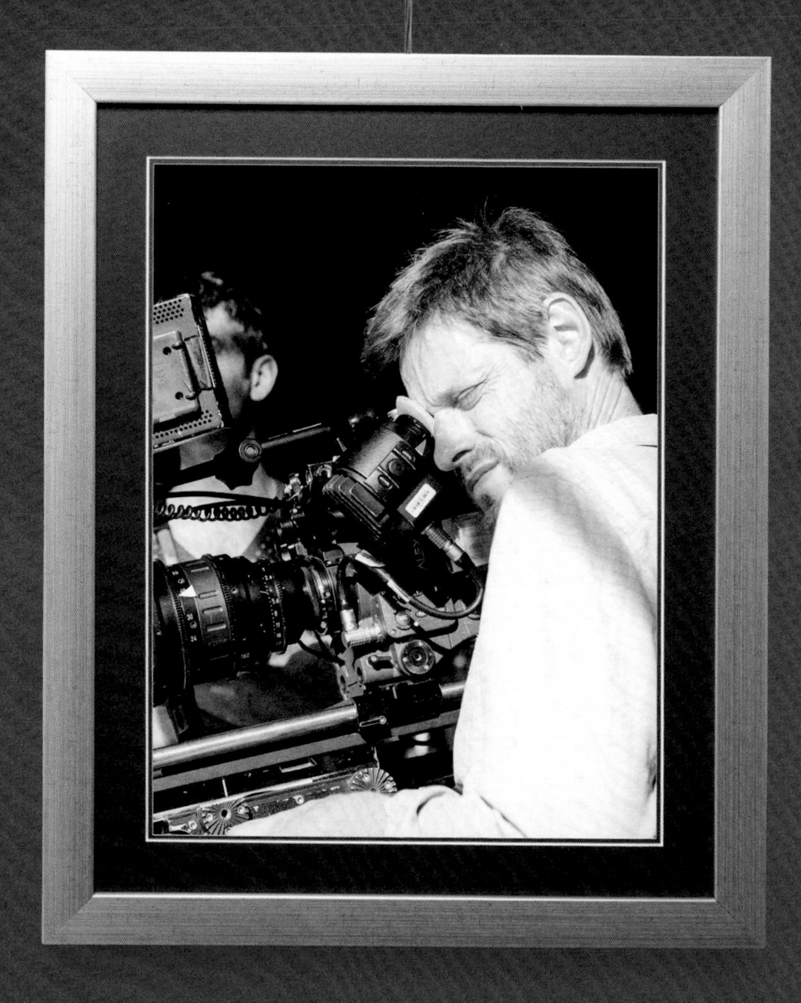

TRISTAN OLIVER

A cinematographer for 26 years, Tristan Oliver has worked across the film disciplines. His long collaboration with director Nick Park includes the Academy award winners *Wrong Trousers, A Close Shave* and *The Curse of the Were-Rabbit*. His work with other directors has produced BAFTA short winners, *Stage Fright* and *The Big Story*, as well as the popular feature films *Chicken Run*, the Academy award nominated *Fantastic Mr. Fox* and *ParaNorman*.Tristan has just wrapped on the live action shoot for *Loving Vincent*, the first fully painted animated movie where live footage is painstakingly overpainted in the style of Van Gogh.

He is currently in pre-production for Wes Anderson's next stop-frame animated feature.

In the field of commercials, he has filmed a number of significant live action/animation mix campaigns most notably for Sony, Becks, Tesco and Tennants. A member of AMPAS & BAFTA, Tristan has sat on the BAFTA Film and Children's committees with responsibility for children's and family film. He has chaired the animation category awards' jury on a number of occasions. Tristan is a graduate of the University of Bristol and Bristol Film School. His early success in winning the BP Kodak and Fuji Student Cinematography prizes led to a short period at the Moscow Film School.

AMPAS: Academy of Motion Picture Arts and Sciences
BAFTA: British Academy of Film and Television Arts

"If there is a Saville Row equivalent for cameras, then Grays of Westminster is it. The shop is more like an elegant living room than a retail establishment and knowledgeable, smart ladies and gentlemen conduct their business effortlessly and with a knowledge and courtesy almost unseen outside a bespoke tailors.

"Having been a committed Nikon user all my adult life, this temple to the marque, which holds some unique pieces, has me pressing my nose, childlike, to the cabinets, revisiting memories of once-loved and long-gone cameras I used to own.

"Grays of Westminster has supplied a very large number of lenses for me for a number of feature films over the years. The speed of delivery, quality of the merchandise and just the sheer pleasure of dealing with someone who completely understands my requirements and still considers a hand-written letter a necessary part of the service ensures my frequent return.

"There is also the question of Gray Levett's clairvoyant abilities: I shall always remember my surprise when shooting a movie in the States. I had had an enormous amount of difficulty sourcing the particular Nikon lenses I wanted from U.S. suppliers. I picked the phone up to Gray. 'Ah, Mr. Oliver,' he said, 'I've been expecting your call....'"

– Tristan Oliver

CHAPTER 15
ROOM WITH A VIEW

It was a book written by Robert Rotoloni called *Nikon Rangefinder Camera – An Illustrated History of the Nikon Rangefinder Cameras, Lenses and Accessories* that was contributory in creating a market for the collecting of Nikon equipment. Robert Rotoloni also founded the Nikon Historical Society[7], which drew a great deal of attention to the vintage Nikon market.

When Grays of Westminster became ….exclusively Nikon in 1992, Gray and his team decided that there should be an area within the business designated for vintage Nikon, and the lower ground floor was opened to celebrate the seventy-fifth anniversary of the formation of Nippon Kogaku. Called the Nippon Kogaku Room, which translates as Japan Optical (the original name of the Nikon Company), it was in essence a museum as well as an outlet for rare and vintage cameras. The range of camera equipment displayed in this room dated from 1948 when the first Nikon One appeared, through to 1980 when the last F2 was made.

There was an enormous amount of interest in the collection of vintage Nikon in the Nippon Kogaku Room as soon as it had opened. Many Nikon devotees visited Grays of Westminster purely to look at the exhibitions of this elegantly displayed vintage equipment whilst on a trip to London.

As well as camera equipment and many former flagship models, over the last thirty years Grays have displayed rare lenses, trench binoculars and microscopes, including military binoculars stamped and made in occupied Japan, a Nikon air camera of 1941 from a reconnaissance plane, the legendary Nikon F known to many round the world as the 'Vietnam camera' and the very first Nikon S3 rangefinder camera which bears the serial number 6300001.

The department in the lower ground floor has since expanded its range to include contemporary and mint condition second-hand Nikon. The second-hand area is brimming with equipment and Grays' policy

F2A
Photomic
Nikkormat
FT3
NIKKOREX
ZOOM-35
F3
INSTRUCTION MANUAL
Nikon
NIKONOS
IV-A
FS
F90
FTN
F5
FM2
Nikon S3
INSTRUCTIONS
F100
NIKON
Instructions
S2
F4
F2SB
Photomic
INSTRUCTION MANUAL
INSTRUCTIONS
FOR USING
Nikon
CAMERA
FT2
INSTRUCTION MANUAL
NIKKOREX
AUTO35
EL
Nikkormat
FM
NIKKOREX
F90X
ニコンＳ４の使い方
Nikon
S4
F6
Instruction Manual
FA
Nikon
SP
INSTRUCTIONS
NIKONOS
III
EL
Nikkormat
INSTRUCTION MANUAL
FE
F-601
FE2
FM3A
INSTRUCTION MANUAL
INSTRUCTIONS
FOR USING
Nikon
CAMERA
NIKONOS-II
INSTRUCTIONS
Nikon
F3
high-eyepoint
F2
Photomic
FULLY AUTOMATIC REFLEX
Nikon F
NIKONOS
INSTRUCTIONS

is to ensure that only the highest quality lenses and bodies are available for purchase. The ground floor is designated for the display and sales of new equipment, as well as stocking thousands of camera accessories. On this floor you will also find a range of standard manuals and users' guides, as well as comprehensive Nikon handbooks and rare editions.

The most recent addition to Grays of Westminster is the Founder's office on the first floor. Opened in July 2013, it is a large period south-facing room and library, with The Houses of Parliament to the left and The Shard in the distance. The walls are covered with framed posters of a variety of films whose production teams or directors have sourced their on-set equipment from Grays of Westminster. These include such films as Tim Burton's *Corpse Bride*, the *Fantastic Mr. Fox, Wallace and Gromit: The Curse of the Were-Rabbit, Chicken Run, ParaNorman, The Box Trolls* and *Shaun the Sheep The Movie, The Pirates! In an Adventure with Scientists!* It also houses signed testimonials and photographs of actors and artists such as Tom Cruise, David Suchet, Bill Nighy, Kate Bush, the late Patrick Macnee and Stanley Kubrick. In addition, there are also framed and signed classic posters of various concerts which reflect Gray's earlier time as a rock photographer.

Gray Levett said, *"To complete the room within the time-period we had given ourselves, we worked long and late hours as a steady procession of carpenters, electricians, window cleaners, painters and carpet fitters arrived. A background symphony of sawing, banging, plugging, unplugging, fitting and testing continued for days like some strange orchestra that was an ever-present companion. At last they finished their work and a pleasant odour of beeswax furniture polish hung in the air together with a blessed silence. The only noise was the hum of the air-conditioning unit."*

The first visitor to the new room was Mr. Junichi Itoh, the Vice-President of the Nikon Corporation, accompanied by Mr. Hidehiko Tanaka, Managing Director of Nikon U.K.. Joining them was Mr. Kazuhiro Okano, Personal Secretary to the President and Ms. Ami Yokoyama, an electronics designer from the Coolpix Division. Itoh-san and his guests spent a pleasant hour touring at Grays of Westminster.

On Friday 28th November 2014, for the first time in the history of Grays of Westminster, Mr. Kazuo Ushida, the President of the Nikon Corporation, visited Grays of Westminster and the offices of Nikon Owner with his team from Japan. He was accompanied by Mr. John Walshe, the general manager of Nikon U.K.. Mr. Kazuo Ushida toured the premises, taking particular interest in Grays of Westminster's vintage and second-hand departments, as well as Grays' extensive history.

In doing so, Mr Kazuo Ushida paid Grays of Westminster a most singular honour. ■

Nikon F55
Nikon F65
AF-S
AF-S
Nikon
CT-200
FOR
NIKKOR ED 200mm f/2
Nikon
Nikon
Nikon
CT-402
Nikon
Nikon F5

The Nippon Kogaku Room

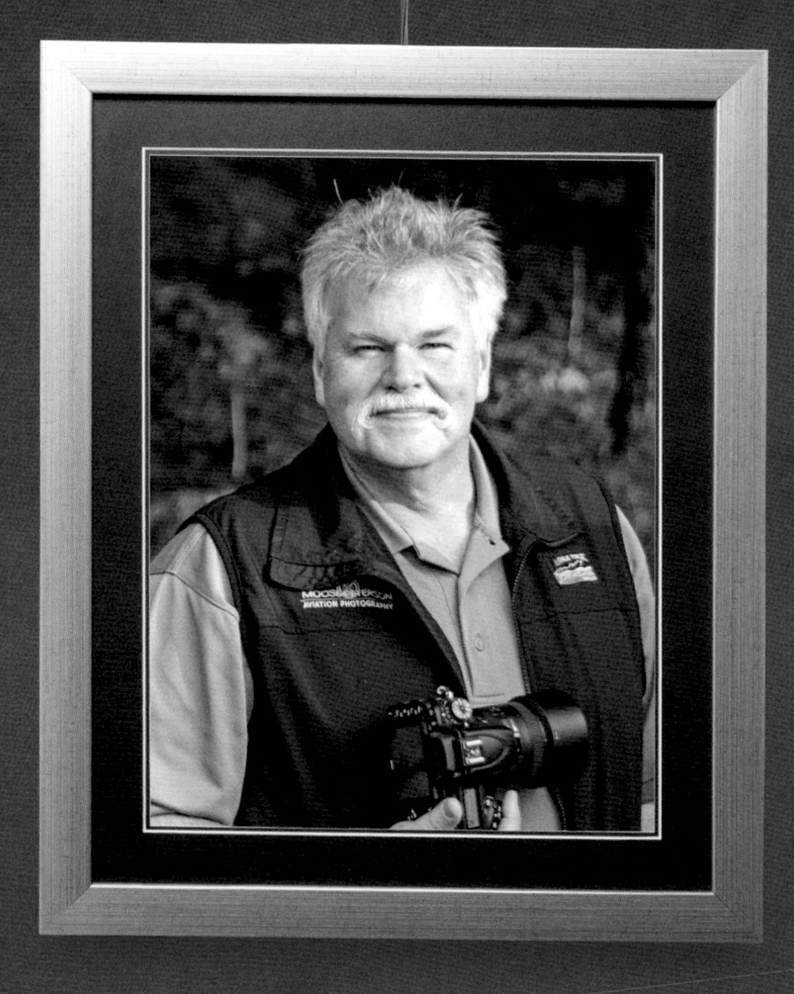

MOOSE PETERSON

Moose Peterson's true passion is wildlife photography and he considers himself incredibly fortunate to be amongst North America's critters and to be able to bring back their stories with his camera. Along the way Moose has also been fortunate to be recognized for his passion: Nikon U.S.A. Ambassador, Lexar Elite Photographer, recipient of the John Muir Conservation Award, Research Associate with the Endangered Species Recovery Program, to name just a few.

He shares his knowledge through his writing and lecturing. He has been published in over 143 magazines worldwide and is the author of 28 books, including *Photographic FUNdamentals*, *Taking Flight* and *Captured*; he has lectured across the country to thousands upon thousands of photographers. One of the original Nikon shooters to receive the D1 in 1999, Moose embraced this new technology becoming the only wildlife photographer in the world to shoot strictly digital in the early years. While a beta site for all the major hardware and software manufacturers, Moose continues his main goal of photographing the life history of North America's endangered wildlife and wild places. Being a creative innovator of new techniques both behind the camera and the computer is the driving force behind his photography and goals. www.moosepeterson.com

"There is this fabled land of myth and lore where Nikons live, and it really exists! If you're into Nikon, I mean really, really, really into Nikon, you know Grays of Westminster.

"It was back in the 1980s when I first talked with Gray Levett of Grays of Westminster about an eclectic, obscure piece of Nikon gear. We have talked and emailed throughout the years enjoying a delightful friendship. Today, Sharon & I had the great fortune to actually spend time with Gray and Gillian at what can only be called the Disneyland of Nikon. You see here the ever-dapper Gray, holding his Nikon F + F-36 motor drive he shot rock bands with back in the 1960s, with the same passion he had back in the day. His knowledge of the Nikon system, the entire system from its very beginning up to the very latest, is simply stunning.

"While Grays of Westminster has all the current gear, what they are so well-known for is their service, knowledge and inventory of classic Nikon gear which includes some of the first ever manufactured in the days of the Nikon Rangefinder and the first SLR. In this case before us were some amazing historic pieces, either one of a kind or very rare items. I found a rare, 10mm f/5.6 OP Fisheye-Nikkor that I had back in the day, a gorgeous circular fisheye that required the mirror up to attach it to a body. It was a marvellous day going through old gear and memories and to come to know so much dearer someone I've known and respected since the first days of my career. And to find new, in the box, original DK-2 eyecups was the icing on the cake! One of the highlights of our London adventure, meeting the Levetts and spending time with them at the store will never be forgotten. It has been an amazing week, all from the blessings of photography, further proving the power of the click to change our world!"

– Moose Peterson

CHAPTER 16
ALL THE GLITTERING PRIZES

Voltaire, the French writer, historian and philosopher said, *"Appreciation is a wonderful thing. It makes what is excellent in others belong to us as well."*

Over the years, The Nikon Corporation and Nikon U.K. have presented Grays of Westminster with a number of prestigious awards.

Grays of Westminster were acknowledged by Nikon with an award in 2003, 2007 and 2009 for their unprecedented sales of Nikon and their contributions to the Nikon brand internationally. In 2010, on the celebration of their 25th anniversary, they were given a beautiful Japanese plate by the current President of Nikon Imaging Mr Yasuyuki Okamoto in recognition of being such a long-standing presence in the photographic industry. At the same time, Nikon U.K. awarded Grays with a stunning, heavy crystal trophy which reads: *"Presented to Grays of Westminster to celebrate their 25th Anniversary and their outstanding contribution to Nikon users."*

These awards were followed in 2013 by a set of exquisite Japanese porcelain presented by Mr. Junichi Itoh, the Vice-President of the Nikon Corporation.

The following year, in November 2014, on his visit to the company, Mr Kazuo Ushida, the President of the Nikon Corporation, personally presented the founder and directors of Grays of Westminster with a beautiful porcelain dish made by Fukagawa-Seiji, purveyors to The Imperial Household. Based in Arita, Japan, the birthplace of Japanese porcelain, they have a history that is over 100 years old. The almost transparent white porcelain is made possible by the use of extremely high temperatures in the firing of each item. The blue colour is so unique that it is called "Fukagawa blue" and is highly sought-after by porcelain collectors. Grays of Westminster also holds the unique distinction of being the only company ever to have won all three Dealer of the Year awards voted by the readers of *Amateur Photographer, Practical Photography* and *Buying Cameras* magazines in one year. In 2011 they won the *Pixel Magazine* Trade Award: Independent Retailer of the Year, and the *What Digital Camera/Amateur Photographer* 'Gold Winner' Good Service Award in 2011, 2012, 2013, 2014 and 2015 as voted for by the public. In addition, they received the 'Gold Good Service Award' voted for by the readers of *Digital Photo* and *Practical Photography* in both 2014 and 2015.

Westminster in Bloom Awards 1994 awarded to Grays of Westminster

Buying Cameras Dealer of the Year Award 1993-1994 awarded to Grays of Westminster

Amateur Photographer Dealer of the Year awarded to Grays of Westminster 1994

Practical Photography Awards 1994 The People's Choice - Grays of Westminster Dealer of the Year

Presented to Grays of Westminster to commemorate their outstanding contribution in promoting the Nikon system. October 2003 - Nikon U.K. Limited and Nikon Corporation Japan

Presented to Grays of Westminster by Nikon to celebrate their unprecedented sales 2007 - Nikon U.K. Limited and Nikon Corporation Japan

50th Anniversary of the Nikon F Award presented to Grays of Westminster for their record-breaking sales 2008/09 by Nikon U.K. Limited

Sales Award - presented by Nikon U.K. - 'Thank you for your contribution to our business in 2010'

Pixel Magazine Trade Award: Grays of Westminster - Independent Retailer of the Year 2011

Presented to Grays of Westminster on their 25th Anniversary by the President of Nikon Japan

PRESENTED TO

on the historic occasion of being
the only camera shop in the world
to be granted their own Coat of Arms by

HER MAJESTY'S COLLEGE OF ARMS

FROM

Nikon
CORPORATION

29th October 2014

What Digital Camera/Amateur Photographer 'Gold Winner' Good Service Award 2011, as voted for by *What Digital Camera* readers and website visitors

Presented to Grays of Westminster to celebrate their 25th Anniversary and their outstanding contribution to Nikon users, 2011 - Nikon U.K. Limited

What Digital Camera/Amateur Photographer 'Gold Winner' Good Service Award 2012, as voted for by *What Digital Camera* readers and website visitors

What Digital Camera/Amateur Photographer 'Gold Winner' Good Service Award 2013, as voted for by *What Digital Camera* readers and website visitors

What Digital Camera/Amateur Photographer 'Gold Retailer' Good Service Award 2014, as voted for by *What Digital Camera* readers and website visitors

Gear of the Year 2014 Gold Service Award, as voted for by *Digital Photo & Practical Photography* magazine readers and website visitors

What Digital Camera/Amateur Photographer 'Gold Retailer' Good Service Award 2015, as voted for by *What Digital Camera* readers and website visitors

Promotion of the Year for the Grays of Westminster Coat of Arms story *BPI News* Trade Awards 2015 Promotion of the Year

Gear of the Year 2015 Gold Service Award, as voted for by *Digital Photo & Practical Photography* magazine readers and website visitors

SIMON STAFFORD

Simon Stafford first became interested in photography while a university student; completely self-taught, he talked his way into a job as the photographer for the university's weekly newspaper and has been shooting pictures ever since.

He has accrued a wealth of experience over the past thirty years in both film and digital photography. During this time he has worked extensively with Nikon equipment; Simon has used Nikon digital SLR cameras exclusively since 2004. The author of more than twenty-five books on the Nikon camera system, he has also presented a wide range of seminars, workshops and lead photography tours in the U.K., Europe, Africa and Asia. Simon also contributes to a number of U.K. photography magazines and is the Technical Editor of *Nikon Owner* magazine.

"Grays of Westminster possesses a reputation, established over many years, which is second to none not only within the UK photographic retail industry, but also much farther afield. It has been built on pillars of exceptional quality of service, and unparalleled range of stock in both new and second-hand Nikon equipment.

"A visit to the shop is an experience in itself, as you are seemingly transported to a bygone era when courtesy, attentive service and customer care were the norm, complimented by the traditional appearance of its interior, which exudes refinement creating a very agreeable ambience. Gray Levett and his staff deliver this level of service in an understated manner, yet it is consistently knowledgeable, meticulous and reassuringly personal. The numerous wooden display cabinets within are filled to the brim with Nikon camera equipment, from the contemporary to items that are decades old and often extremely rare; such is the variety of items on view that perusing their contents enables you to trace the history and development of the Nikon marque from its earliest origins to the present day. In short, Grays of Westminster is a unique phenomenon in the world of photography: a bountiful and highly satisfying emporium for any photographer who appreciates Nikon equipment.

"On a personal note it has been a pleasure and a privilege to be associated with Grays of Westminster for almost a quarter of a century, first as a customer, but soon thereafter as an occasional contributor to the Grays of Westminster Gazette, which led subsequently to my current involvement with Nikon Owner magazine as Technical Editor. Over the years I have met many people through Grays: staff, customers, members of the Nikon Corporation, and people working in the photographic industry worldwide. I consider myself very fortunate to now count a good number of them as friends."

– Simon Stafford

CHAPTER 17 THE GRAYS OF WESTMINSTER 'COAT OF ARMS'

On October 29th, 2014 Grays of Westminster were granted their own Coat of Arms by the Lancaster Herald at the Institute of Directors, London, becoming the first camera shop in the world to receive this distinction.

The Coat of Arms as a heraldic tradition has a distinguished history, fashioned by honour and knightly deeds, lyrical identity and brightly-wrought emblems. Yet the legend behind the first significant Coat of Arms in England was perhaps defined most of all by the ever-shifting climate of politics and power of the Middle Ages.

The year was 1128, over six decades since that fateful date in English history, the Battle of Hastings, 14th October 1066. This was an age of sovereign rule and medieval hierarchy, bound by the rules of unwavering loyalty and personal fealty; yet it was also a time of conflict, with passions running high and rivalries forged by long-held feuds and disputes. Henry I of England, the fourth son of William the Conqueror, had been on the throne since 1100, following decades of royal feuds, dark treacheries and rampant duplicity, sibling rivalry taken to its most extreme. Conspiracy theories on how he inherited the throne, even then, were rife.

The crepuscular world that King Henry's subjects inhabited was grim and unpredictable. Life was often nasty, brutish and short, and royal weddings and an orderly line of succession provided cohesion and stability, as well as an increased perception of majesty. These unions were almost always fashioned by the geopolitics of the moment, creating alliances and strengthening allegiance, an integral factor in

> "...THE LEGEND BEHIND THE FIRST SIGNIFICANT COAT OF ARMS IN ENGLAND WAS PERHAPS DEFINED MOST OF ALL BY THE EVER-SHIFTING CLIMATE OF POLITICS AND POWER OF THE MIDDLE AGES.

the continuance of the dynastic line and the maintenance of peace within the realm.

When Henry arranged the marriage between his widowed daughter Matilda and Geoffrey of Anjou, according to legend, he presented Geoffrey with a badge of gold lions. This would not have been some casual gift, but an important visual embodiment of anticipated allegiance, a sort of twelfth-century insurance policy for the future. It is this very honour, a blue shield emblazoned with gold lions, which has been considered by many to be the earliest recorded royal bestowal of a Coat of Arms in the kingdom, and from where the origins of English heraldic identification might be found.

In time, Coats of Arms and their colourful emblems came into general practice in order to identify lords and knights on a battlefield, to define the spirit of valour and true-heartedness. During subsequent centuries, the concept was expanded to include families of the higher orders of society and their successive generations, ultimately making way for the distinguished body of heraldry and other bearings and insignia that can be found currently.

Today, for any person or organisation to have a legal right to a Coat of Arms, it has to be granted to them by the Earl Marshal, the 18th Duke of Norfolk, through the Herald at the College of Arms in London. Heralds are appointed by The Queen and are delegated to act on her behalf in all concerns of heraldry and the granting of new Coats of Arms.

The criteria that is taken into account before a Coat of Arms is granted might include such things as awards or honours from the Crown, public and charitable services, or eminence and good standing in national or local life. Coats of Arms are painted on vellum using ink and 22-carat gold paint decorated by a herald painter, with the text written by a scrivener, the whole process taking a year to create. The College of Arms maintains an ancient English tradition of manuscript writing and illumination which can be traced back to early monastic scriptoria.

Almost nine centuries have passed and the world of knights and barons, of fiercely-fought wars and bloody feuds have disappeared; only faint ghosts of those battles linger in our collective memory, drifting disembodied through the mists and fabric of history.

Yet the heraldic statement of that most singular of creations, the Coat of Arms and its visually powerful symbols and emblems, continues to exist. Just as importantly, so too does the renown and valour the Coat of Arms bestows.

The concept of Grays of Westminster is most aptly embodied within the motto of their Coat of Arms: *Lead in Order to Serve*, or in Latin, *Praesis ut Prosis.* ■

"

THE CONCEPT OF GRAYS OF WESTMINSTER IS MOST APTLY EMBODIED WITHIN THE MOTTO OF THEIR COAT OF ARMS: *LEAD IN ORDER TO SERVE*, OR IN LATIN, *PRAESIS UT PROSIS*.

GRANTING THE GRAYS OF WESTMINSTER 'COAT OF ARMS' BY ROBERT NOEL, LANCASTER HERALD

In principle, a coat of arms comprises the Arms of The Queen, those of the Earl Marshal and of the College of Arms as well as the Armorial Bearings of the recipient, a blazon which is a formal description of the coat of arms, a pennant, a badge, a shield and a motto.

The heralds are appointed by the British Sovereign and are the delegated authority to act on The Queen's behalf in all matters of heraldry and the granting of new coats of arms. Robert Noel, The Lancaster Herald, explains how the Grays of Westminster Coat of Arms was made and also includes a brief explanation of the symbolism used.

"Once the Earl Marshal, the 18th Duke of Norfolk, had issued his Warrant of Approval for the Grays of Westminster Coat of Arms, the preparation was put in hand.

"The Coat of Arms was executed on vellum measuring approximately 24 inches by 18 inches. The vellum was finished by rubbing it with a combination of powdered pumice stone and a very fine wet-and-dry sanding sheet, and then burnished, the ensuing contoured surface of the vellum being capable of miraculous longevity.

"Across the heading of the Coat of Arms there is an illumination in full colour of the Arms of The Queen flanked by those of the Earl Marshal and of the College of Arms. The Armorial Bearings of Grays of Westminster were similarly emblazoned in the upper left-hand part of the Letters Patent. The blazon of the Armorial Bearings was added to the body of the document which was then signed by the three Kings of Arms: Garter Principal King of Arms, Clarenceux King of Arms, and Norroy and Ulster King of Arms who also attached to the Patent their seals of office which hang from the document by means of corded silk ribbons and are contained in metal seal boxes.

"A brief explanation of some of the symbolism within the image of the Coat of Arms follows. The Lion, symbolising Gray Levett, is amicably communing with the bird of Japan, the green pheasant. The mural crown around its neck stands for responsibility to the public. Its right paw is resting on a camera lens. The cornucopia representing flourishing growth is replenished with flowers and represents the various facets of Grays of Westminster. These flowers include Hampshire purslane and the Dorset heath flowers of the Hampshire/Dorset borders, where Gillian Greenwood and Gray Levett were born and brought up, and Rhododendron Rothschildii, the unofficial 'Tel Aviv's city flower', in a reference to Tel Aviv having

L-R: Thomas Woodcock Somerset Herald, Sir Peter Gwynn-Jones Garter King of Arms, Robert Noel Blue Mantle Pursuivant (now Lancaster Herald)

been the birthplace of Uri Zakay. The addition of the Christmas rose within the design is to recall The Christmas Shop in Southwark which gave Gray Levett the idea of dealing with one brand only - Nikon. The tip of the horn has been modelled into an emblematic portcullis for Westminster. The rays of light emanating behind the flowers symbolise the derivation of the word photography, which derives from photo (light) and graphy (writing). The rationale of the badge is an occidental phoenix but it has two heads for looking both east and west. The phoenix symbolises the energy of growing trade and the friendly relationships of trade. The 'house colours' of Grays of Westminster are blue and gold and the badge is in those colours.

"The Motto, Lead In Order To Serve, emphasises 'service' and the concept of Grays of Westminster being a leader in its field (Latin: Praesis Ut Prosis)." ■

"THE MOTTO, *LEAD IN ORDER TO SERVE*, EMPHASISES 'SERVICE' AND THE CONCEPT OF GRAYS OF WESTMINSTER BEING A LEADER IN ITS FIELD...

Armorial bearing: heraldry consisting of a design or image depicted on a shield.
Vellum: parchment made from the skin of an animal.
Letters patent: a type of legal instrument in the form of a published written order issued by a monarch or president, generally granting an office, right, monopoly, title or status to a person or corporation.
Cornucopia: A symbol of food and abundance dating back to the 5th century BC, also referred to as 'horn of plenty' or 'harvest cone', usually filled with fruits and corn etc..

DAVID SUCHET, CBE

David Suchet is best-known as Agatha Christie's suave Belgian super-sleuth Hercule Poirot in a role spanning three decades. Early on in his career, the legendary London-born actor enjoyed many roles as Shakespearean villains such as Iago in *Othello*, Tybalt in *Romeo and Juliet* and Caliban in *The Tempest*. David Suchet has played the part of a Middle Eastern terrorist in *The Little Drummer Girl* (1984), a Russian operative in *The Falcon* and the *Snowman* (1985), a French hunter in *Harry and the Hendersons* (1987), a Polish bishop in *To Kill a Priest* (1988) and Napoleon himself in *Sabotage!* (2000). He also took on some masterful television roles portraying a number of historical, biblical and entertainment figures, including Sigmund Freud in the mini-series *Freud* (1984), news reporter William L. Shirer in the biopic *Murrow* (1986), Aaron in *Moses* (1995), and movie mogul Louis B. Mayer in *RKO 281* (1999). He has given potent, award-winning performances on the non-Shakespearean stage, particularly his George in *Who's Afraid of Virginia Woolf?* in 1996 and, from 1998 to 2001, composer Salieri in *Amadeus*, which he took to Broadway and for which he received a Tony nomination. More recently, he played Cardinal Wolsey in *Henry VIII* (2003) and the vampire nemesis *Van Helsing in Dracula* (2006). In 2007 he played Cardinal Benelli in *The Last Confession*, about the death of Pope John Paul 1 in 1978. He reprised the role of Benelli in a world tour from April to October 2014 and starred as Lady Bracknell in *The Importance of Being Earnest* by Oscar Wilde at the Vaudeville Theatre in London in June 2015. He is also a very keen photographer.

"To all the persons of Grays of Westminster.

"I would like to take this opportunity to say "merci beaucoup" for all the kindnesses and the many occasions of advise that you have afforded to me.

"I have to say that the taking of the photographs with the Nikon F90 is an experience most pleasurable. It seems to posses very many excellent little grey cells of its own which allows mine to have the little rest. Of course when I wish that my own should have the exercise I can make use of the little switch which is used for the rotations and then I take full control.

"Also when it is very dark my excellent SB-25 flash is just superb – just as intelligent as the camera. En effet, there are times when I wonder if my presence is necessary at all!

"With many felicitations."

– Hercule Poirot

From a hand-written letter on Hercule Poirot's personal stationery from the world-famous television series. This can be seen on display at Grays of Westminster.

CHAPTER 18 GRAYS OF WESTMINSTER, A SHOP FOR ALL SEASONS

Over the last few years, Grays of Westminster have taken on the additional role of specialised consultancy, as more and more often they have been approached to act as experts in the area of Nikon equipment; they are, for example, often approached by publishers all over the world to edit and check prestigious books on specific Nikon equipment for accuracy.

Over the years, they have supplied equipment for animated films (as mentioned in Chapter 15) such as Tim Burton's *Corpse Bride, The Fantastic Mr. Fox, Wallace and Gromit: The Curse of the Were-Rabbit, Chicken Run, ParaNorman, Metro Manila, The Box Trolls, Shaun The Sheep The Movie* and *Kubo and the Two Strings.* The are also frequently approached by directors of photography who might be working on a film, a television production or other live-action piece, as to which manual focus lenses would be most suitable for use in a particular production. In addition, Grays are regularly asked for advice as Nikon specialists about the correct choice of photographic equipment to be used in a television series or in a film which might be set in a contemporary period or an earlier era.

In July 2002, Grays of Westminster, represented by Gray Levett, was invited by Heather McGlone, the editor of the *Daily Mail Weekend* magazine, to assist with a photographic competition entitled *A Weekend in Great Britain.*

Grays of

The idea of the competition was to capture the essence of a weekend in Britain in picture form. Gray Levett was asked to join a panel of experts headed by a member of The Royal Family, Lord Lichfield, Britain's leading royal photographer Tim Graham, artist and photographer Christiane Kubrick, widow of the film director Stanley Kubrick, portrait photographer Kay Hartenstein Saatchi and Simon Stafford, technical editor of *Nikon Owner* magazine. Gray Levett arranged the prize of £7,000 worth of Nikon camera equipment with Nikon U.K.. The competition was featured, together with a variety of photographic articles, over a period of two weekends. Both Gray Levett and Simon Stafford were interviewed to give their advice on how photographers could get the best out of their cameras. They also discussed what defines effective composition: how to recognise it, how to utilise and perfect it. Over three thousand people entered the competition.

The results of the competition were published in a four-page article in the *Daily Mail Weekend* magazine in August 2003. This was followed more recently in 2014 by another photographic competition in the *Daily Mail Weekend* magazine entitled the Great British Wildlife Photography Competition; Gray Levett and Simon Stafford were again on the team of judges, which included Michela Strachan, from BBC's *Autumnwatch* and *Springwatch*, Kate Humble who has presented *Animal Park, Springwatch, Autumnwatch, Wild in Africa* and *Seawatch*, author and presenter Chris Packham of *The Really Wild Show* and *Springwatch*, as well as BAFTA-winning English naturalist Steve Backshall, who was part of the expedition teams in *Lost Land of the Tiger, Lost Land of the Volcano* and *Lost Land of the Jaguar.* The competition was a huge success, with many thousands of people entering, and the winning entries were exhibited at the Strand Gallery in London.

The competition was repeated in 2015, and both Gray Levett and Simon Stafford returned as judges for the Great British Wildlife Photography Challenge with the panel of judges which included Ben Fogle, the distinguished broadcaster, traveller and writer, Bill Oddie, presenter of various wildlife shows such as *Bill Oddie Goes Wild* and *Springwatch, Countryfile* presenter Ellie Harrison, conservationist and co-host of *Springwatch*, Martin Hughes-Games, and Philippa Forrester, the former *Tomorrow's World* presenter, who has also hosted BBC shows such as *Making Animal Babies*. Both Gray and Simon were interviewed to give their advice on how photographers could get the best out of their cameras, and when Gray was asked to cast his expert eyes over the entries, he said that he was stunned at the standard of the submissions each year, and that the junior entries were as exceptional as the adults'.

Nikon
Binoculars
Nikon
FIELDMICROSCOPE
Portable 20x stereoscopic microscope
Nikon
F5
CONTROLS
Comprehensive operation system
Nikon
F90X
Higher speed, greater accuracy
THINK AGAIN
YOU CAN START
Nikon
28Ti
35Ti
Grays of Westminster
Exclusively...Nikon
The Catalogue
1997
Nikon FM2
Nikon FE10
35mm (135) Format SLR with Automatic Exposure Control
Nikon F3
F3 high-eyepoint
The
Grays of Westminster
Nikon
F90X
Higher speed, greater accuracy

THE GRAYS OF WESTMINSTER CATALOGUE

From 1992 until 2000 Grays of Westminster produced a series of mail-order catalogues describing their services and listing all their equipment and accessories in the Nikon range, together with the prices.

These catalogues would appear in the summer and winter of each year. Each of the catalogues was designed individually to convey a certain atmosphere, and with their rich Oxford Blue covers and gold lettering, they have become collectable items.

Gray based the design for these on the catalogue from Fribourg & Treyer, one of London's oldest tobacconists and purveyors of snuff, established in 1720.

FRIBOURG & TREYER

Grays of Westminster
Exclusively... Nikon

Winter Catalogue
Pimlico London

When Grays of Westminster released their 1994 Winter Catalogue Gray Levett approached an old friend, the distinguished writer, poet, performer Robin Williamson[8], to write something for the catalogue with Midwinter and Christmas in mind.

He wrote the following piece *"Here's to Midwinter"* that vividly conjures up the winter season.

Here's to Midwinter

By Robin Williamson

Standing again at the crossroads
of Winter here's to midwinter
and the twinkle of bright eyes
and here's to me Tom Fool
with my handful of holly
I'll write the wren boys in, in frosty Antrim
& the Welsh with the Mari Llwyd[9]
I'll write a twinkle in those eye holes
in the lanes of Ceredigion

Claret faced Christmas
talking turkey will have its full say
with carols till your ears melt

but I'll write magic
in a star hung sky
and what the wind whispers
on the black roadside nowhere
where the dead & the unborn
listen whispers this:
every kiss should be about what will be
every tear must be for what will never
come again

here's to midwinter and the twinkle of bright eyes
here's to what cannot be taken
from the lowest in the coldest doorway
here's to what the highest cannot keep
with the highest walls
here's to what the granny and the wee baby knows
here's to the heart beat of the world
and here's to you.

Nikon
Grays of Westminster
Exclusively... Nikon

THE GRAYS OF WESTMINSTER F5 PAPERWEIGHT

When Nikon introduced the launch of the new flagship F5, Grays of Westminster was keen to commemorate the event.

Nikon make over two hundred types of their own optical glass, so in conjunction with Nikon Japan, Grays of Westminster ordered a rather special Nikon F5 paperweight. The word paperweight is not quite the correct description as the item was a finely polished chunk of genuine Nikon optical glass.

Gray Levett originally approached Nikon with the plan to produce a special Grays of Westminster paperweight carrying the distinctive shop logo. The former Japanese Liaison, Toru Iwaoka, made the suggestion of incorporating within the design a picture of the new flagship F5 camera.

Thanks to the assistance of Mr. Iwaoka, and with some help from a number of contacts at the Nikon Corporation, a fine piece of optical art was produced. This was of great historical interest as it featured the new F5 and included the distinctive Grays of Westminster logo as well as being the very first collaboration of its kind.

Grays of Westminster ordered one hundred of these very special paperweights, which sold out within a matter of days upon arrival from Japan. ■

CHRIS WESTON

Chris Weston became a professional wildlife photographer in 2001 in order to follow his passion for what he describes as 'the extraordinary behaviour of wildlife'. His contemporary approach to photography led to *Amateur Photographer* magazine describing him as 'One of the most dynamic wildlife photographers working today.' He specializes in photographing mammals and endangered species and is renowned for his ability to connect with wildlife and reveal the often hidden personalities of his subjects through his images.

His work is published globally, with clients including the BBC, ITV, *The Daily Telegraph, The Independent, The Guardian* and *National Geographic*. He has written over 30 books on photography and wildlife and in 2011 his images were selected by *The Sunday Times* magazine for its feature titled *'The Year's Best Animal Photographs'*.

Chris's work is driven by conservation. In 2009, he published the iconic book *Animals on the Edge: Reporting from the Frontline of Extinction,* which has been described as 'The most up-to-date visual survey of our world's rare and endangered species.' He was named by *Outdoor Photography* magazine as one of the world's '40 Most Influential' wildlife photographers.
http://chrisweston.photography

"A while ago, I was sitting with Gray in his beautifully appointed office talking about the exquisiteness of the Japanese tea ceremony – chanoyu (茶の湯). In particular, I was extolling the virtues, which centre on mindfulness, around which the ceremony is performed.

"Chanoyu has little to do with drinking tea. The ceremony is all about aesthetics. Every movement of the carefully choreographed ritual is performed artfully, from the heart. Every gesture is made in consideration of the unique needs of each shokyaku (guest).

"On this occasion, like most visitors to Grays of Westminster, I wasn't calling in for tea. I was there on business. However, as we talked, the parallels to be found in the conversation were not lost on me.

"To experience the legendary service on which Grays' reputation is built is like taking pleasure in the attentiveness of chanoyu. Just as chanoyu has little to do with drinking tea, visiting Grays is an event of which the purchase is only a minor part of the process. At this point, I could wax lyrical about the oak panelling and the leather chairs that hark back to a grander day in retail; equally, I could talk about the vast range of equipment on display and the wealth of knowledge that every member of staff possesses.

"All of these qualities are true and in abundance. But there is something else about Grays of Westminster that makes it special and that is, as it is with chanoyu, the energy that encompasses the experience.

"Energy plays a significant and important role in my photography. When I am in the heart of nature's wildness, my Nikon camera in my hands, focused on whichever critter is the centre of my attention, I am completely aware – mindful – of the moment. It is the process – the whole process – that enables me to receive the images I make. The photograph is because of what went before.

"And so it is at Grays of Westminster, where service is an art form, something to be performed from the heart and in complete mindfulness of the individual. In so being, the ambience connects you deeply with all that you're surrounded by, creating a profound satisfaction that leads to the knowledge that the camera in your hand is because of what went into it being there."

– Chris Weston

CHAPTER 19
PROFESSIONALISM & PERFECTIONISM

The distinguished photographer Tony Hurst works regularly with Grays of Westminster creating beautiful and professional images of Nikon equipment which have been featured over a number of years in many of Grays of Westminster's iconic advertisements in the photographic press, in *Nikon Owner* magazine, as well as the long-running *Grays of Westminster Gazette.*

Gray Levett's first introduction to Tony Hurst was through his famous back covers featuring Nikon cameras and equipment in the *Journal* of the Nikon Historical Society.

His stunning images of vintage and contemporary Nikon camera equipment create an emotional reaction in everyone who views them. By seamlessly fusing light and form, shadow and texture to create a powerful narrative, the pictures he creates are not simply monotone records of the equipment but graceful, reflective portraits of cameras and lenses.

They are almost painterly in aspect, each with the appearance and attention to detail of a still life by an Old Master. Such is the quality of Tony's work, that English photographer and film-director, the late great Terence Donovan[10], described him as a genius.

A selection of Tony Hurst's black and white photographs is permanently displayed at Grays of Westminster in London.

On the following pages you will also find an array of his work. ■

5cm f/1.1 Nikkor RF

Nikon FEA Camera

Nikon F Apollo

Nikon FA Gold

5cm f/3.5 Micro-Nikkor RF

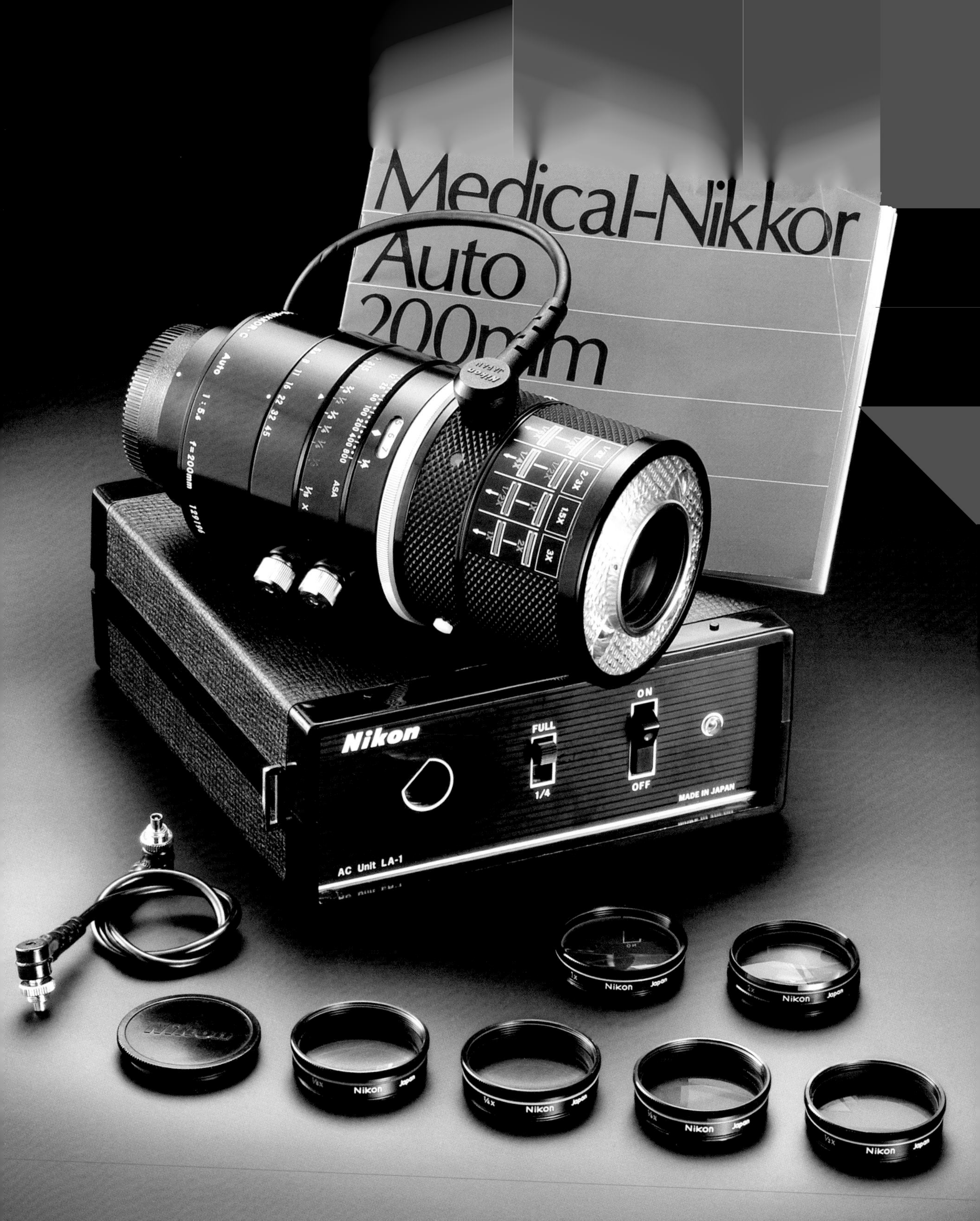

200mm f/5.6 Medical-Nikkor Outfit

Nikon F Apollo plus F-250
Exposure Motor Drive Back

10mm f/5.6 OP
Fisheye-Nikkor

Early Nikon F on a unique stand designed by
Tony Hurst and made by Michael Eleftheriades

6mm f/2.8 Fisheye-Nikkor

13mm f/5.6 Nikkor AIS

Nikon F
No. 6500000

Nikon F2SB Photomic

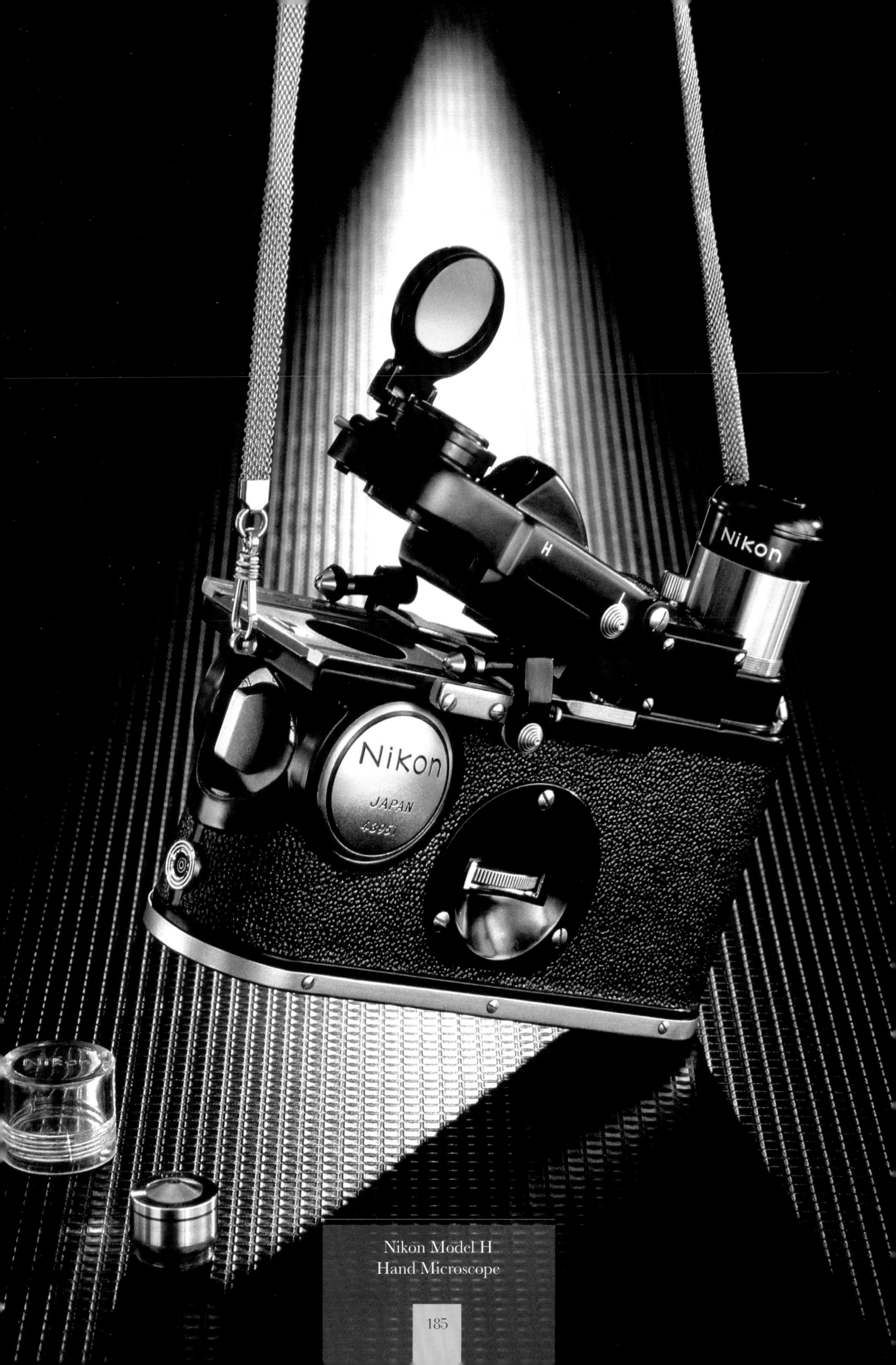

Nikon Model H
Hand Microscope

Nikon FM2 Lapita

Nikon F Photomic FTn

Nikon F + F-36 motor drive, early Nikkor lenses & voltmeter

Nikon FM2 Year of the Dragon
Millennium Edition

Nikon Microflex Outfit

Nikon SP camera & RF lenses,
Varifocal finder and filters

Nikon F3 NASA

Nikon Varifocal Finder

Nikon Model One

Nikon M unsynched

ANDREW MAIN WILSON

Andrew Main Wilson joined AMBA as Chief Executive in 2013. AMBA is the world's leading MBA Organisation, accrediting the top 2% of Executive MBA Business Schools globally and is a membership organisation for the world leaders of tomorrow, servicing MBA members in over 100 countries worldwide.

Prior to joining AMBA, Andrew was Chief Operating Officer of the Institute of Directors, the Marketing Director & Commercial Director of Thomas Cook and Sales & Marketing Director of Citibank Diners Club.

Andrew has a passion for troubleshooting and rejuvenating 'intelligent customer' and luxury goods premium brands. He is a Non-Executive Director of Thomas Lyte, and founded the small, luxury holiday brand, Penthouse Holidays.

Andrew also has a strong interest in global leadership excellence. As an interviewer and presenter, he has interviewed many of the world's most influential leaders of the 20th and 21st centuries, including Bill Gates, Lady Thatcher, HRH The Duke of Edinburgh, Archbishop Desmond Tutu and Jack Welch. As a professional travel photographer, he has visited 162 of the world's 200 countries, culminating in a series of articles for *Nikon Owner* magazine.

Andrew was educated at Dulwich College and the University of Birmingham in England and the Harvard Business School in the U.S.A..

"My love affair with – and worldwide dependence on – Nikon bodies and lenses began with the birth of the Nikon F4 in 1987. I handed over a large cheque and in return the photographic retailer handed over a large pile of Nikon boxes. Although it was my first Nikon, it was obvious I actually knew more about the F4 and the Nikkor lens range than the retailer did. No insightful advice. No offer of after sales support. No passion. No nothing.

"I had recently embarked on a global photographic journey to visit every country on Earth and shoot and write the story of the world's greatest travel experiences, in each and every one of them. So I vowed that I would search high and low to find a photographic retailer whose passion for photography, Nikon product knowledge and customer care excellence would become a priceless support to me, from the North Pole to the South Pole, from Albania to Zimbabwe.

"I'd admired the stylish Grays of Westminster advertisements in several U.K. photographic magazines and went to meet Gray Levett in his Aladdin's Cave of new and second-hand Nikon equipment. I finally decided to switch from film to digital when Nikon launched the D2X and the advice and support from Grays was simply astonishing. My first-ever digital shoot was in Tallinn, the capital of Estonia and I needed to urgently resolve a technical problem on a Saturday morning. I rang Grays and not only did they solve the problem, but they called me back an hour later to check how the shoot was progressing!

"Earlier in my career, I was Marketing Director of Thomas Cook. I arranged several events to celebrate the 150th anniversary of Thomas Cook – effectively 150 years since he created the world's first-ever package holiday in 1841. Thomas Cook was passionate about customer service and demonstrated astonishing attention to detail. Gray Levett reminds me very much of Thomas Cook – they even look alike! I learned at Thomas Cook that if you really want to stand out as a retailer, in an increasingly competitive and global world, you need to consistently offer customers three essentials:

1. *Greater product knowledge than your customers.*
2. *An infectious passion for customer service, particularly after-sales service.*
3. *Comprehensive product range and instant availability.*

"Grays of Westminster continues to excel at all of these – the staff's product knowledge, even down to accessories such as eye-cups and filters, is astonishing. The team's genuine interest in customers never seems to wane and their Nikon new and second-hand product range beats any other camera store I have seen, anywhere in the world. I feel inspired whenever I walk into the Pimlico store. Photography, together with travel and sport, is one of the world's three largest lifestyle pursuits, yet most camera stores merely display almost identical ranges of camera bodies and lenses, unimaginatively on shelves. That experience is not much more enticing than walking into a pharmacy.

"When trying to visit every country on Earth, I need to travel light and never risk checking any camera equipment into the luggage hold of an aircraft. So my trust in and dependence on Nikon equipment and Grays of Westminster's after-sales support is huge. Having now completed shoots in 162 countries, I'm eternally grateful that neither Nikon nor Grays have ever let me down. Here's to another 30 years of legendary service and expertise...."

– Andrew Main Wilson
Chief Executive – The Association of MBAs (AMBA)

CHAPTER 20
PAST, PRESENT AND FUTURE: LEGEND & LEGACY

"You are never too old to set another goal or to dream a new dream."
– C.S. Lewis

Little known in England, but deeply respected in Japan, William Adams of Limehouse, the 'English Samurai', was the very first Englishman to set foot in Japan in 1600. A remarkable Elizabethan mariner and an inspirational figure, Adams went on to command a dazzling position in the Japanese court. He was spokesman, adviser and teacher, maintaining an unprecedented friendship with the Shogun[11] and for a time he helped open up Japan to the outside world.

William Adams

In an interesting juxtaposition of events and some four centuries later, it is the combined brilliance of Nikon's engineering and technical skills, their ability to innovate and to continually perceive and create new products, which has conversely opened up the photographic world to Japan.

Likewise, in a few, but very extraordinary years, a special relationship has been cultivated between Grays of Westminster, a very English company, and Nikon, a very Japanese one.

Nikon as well have had a similar goal of exceptional achievement. Each camera or lens, from its conception to its inception on the production line, is a work of art, a point of integrity, carefully crafted with a time-honoured reverence lost in the vicissitudes of our preoccupied, sometimes chaotic world of the twenty-first century.

At Grays of Westminster, the directors and each of the staff individually and together strive towards the goal of providing the customer with the best service that could possibly be attained.

The legacy of human achievement has long since played an important role in society.

Within its framework lies the innate sense of the worth of the individual and of valued deeds; we comprehend that this sort of accomplishment touches us and enriches all of our lives.

Such a legacy and the inspiration it provides is not the exclusive territory of the artist, the writer, the inventor or explorer and can be the measure of any endeavour if created with vision and good intention.

“ GRAYS OF WESTMINSTER, ONE OF MY FAVOURITE PLACES IN THE WHOLE WORLD.

The commonality lies perhaps in the veracity of the undertaking, the way we perceive it universally with our hearts and minds and the immutable timelessness of its objective.

For Grays of Westminster, the principles they aspire to, intrinsic to their undeniable purpose of integrity and exemplary service, are part of both the legacy they bestow and the new goals they create for the future.

I would like to close with the words of legendary nature photographer, environmentalist and filmmaker Jim Brandenburg:

"Grays of Westminster, one of my favourite places in the whole world." ■

40
Grays of Westminster
AUTHORISED DEALER
Nikon
40
AUTHORISED
DEALER
42
40
Grays of Westminster
Nikon
40
Tel: 020 7828 4925
Nikon

RICHARD YOUNG

Richard Young is at the forefront of celebrity photography. With a career spanning over 40 years, and no sign of stopping anytime soon, Richard's exceptional eye and unique approach has cemented him as the most trusted and prolific contemporary photographer to the stars. As both a portraitist and photojournalist, his unerring ability to capture the moment and present a candid, inside view into the world of celebrity has resulted in iconic images that are celebrated in publications throughout the world.

Richard has photographed a diverse and distinguished range of famous celebrities, capturing some genuinely unique moments over the course of his career; for example, he took the last photograph of Keith Moon at a party with Paul and Linda McCartney, just hours before he died. Richard visited orphanages in Romania with Michael Jackson, photographed Sting's wedding to Trudie Styler and toured the country with the Sex Pistols. He has covered parties for the Cannes film festival and the Oscars in Los Angeles. He accompanied and documented United States troops in Iraq and Fidel Castro in Cuba. These examples are only a few of Richard's diverse achievements, and are a mark of the trust that he inspires in his subjects.

"The most important thing for any professional purchasing the tools of his trade is an assurance that the retailer he approaches knows about the product in depth and would at the same time be happy to listen to the purchaser's requirements.

"When I first started going to Grays of Westminster as a devoted Nikon user, I felt that I had finally found a place where someone was willing to listen to my requirements and understand fully what I needed in the way of photographic equipment. Here, at last, was somewhere I would be given both the opportunity to be able to explain what my particular needs were and the time to discuss the most suitable equipment for my shoot.

"Stepping into Grays of Westminster is like going into a Bentley dealership in Berkeley Square, London. Unlike many other retail outlets there is no sales pressure whatsoever, and the generous helpfulness from all the staff is unparalleled. Over the years, I have built a close relationship with Gray Levett and the team at Grays, and because of the unparalleled service I have always received, I have widely recommended Grays of Westminster to many other Nikon devotees, for example Lord Snowdon. There was the time, for instance, that I started using the special Nikon flash bracket, the SK-6A Power Bracket, on the side of my Nikon DSLR camera. It was so new no one else had seen it. When I arrived at various film premiers to do a shoot, the other press photographers asked me "Richard, where did you get that bracket?" I told them there was only one place to buy it from and that was Grays of Westminster.

"Grays of Westminster is a one camera brand outlet. I believe this in itself gives Nikon enthusiasts confidence as I know they're not going to get confused or distracted by other brands, which can easily occur in other camera shops. I work with one brand only, which is Nikon, and for me Nikon is and always has been the ultimate camera system. I started my professional career with a Nikon F Photomic FTn camera, which was thrust into my hands in the spring of 1974. This camera will be with me always.

"When you are working under pressure as a professional photographer, not only do you have to rely on your camera equipment being the best in terms of quality but you also have to have complete certainty that it will not let you down. I feel like that about both Nikon and Grays of Westminster. I know that no matter where I am in the world, no matter what day of the week it is, no matter what time of the night it is, I can call this extraordinary shop in Pimlico, London, and they will deal with my request with a friendly, unruffled calm that has made them so well-loved. I'm delighted and honoured to be able to be part of this fascinating journey through their history. I would not dream of going to another camera store anywhere else for my Nikon."

– Richard Young

DEFINITIONS

Exits and Entrances: All the world's a stage, / And all the men and women merely players; / They have their exits and their entrances: William Shakespeare, *As You Like It*, Act II Scene VII.

[1]**Camera Obscura:** A *camera obscura* (Latin: 'dark chamber') is an optical device that led to photography and the photographic camera. (The device consists of a box or room with a hole in one side.)

[2]**collodion:** the collodion process is an early photographic process, invented by Frederick Scott Archer. It was introduced in the 1850s and by the end of that decade it had almost entirely replaced the first practical photographic process, the daguerreotype.

[3]**There is a history in all men's lives:** William Shakespeare, Henry IV, Part II, Act III, Scene 1.

[4]**The Picture of Forry and Gray:** a pun on the title of *The Picture of Dorian Gray*, a novel by Oscar Wilde.

[5]**osier beds:** an osier bed is a place where osier, a species of willow, is grown for basket-making.

[6]**The regional groups** include a Central London Group, which is run by Michael Eleftheriades (originally Steve Hughes and Robert Sanger), a South-Coast Group run by Adrian Cochrane and Andrew Hewson, an Essex Group run by Andrew Roast, a South-East Group with events that have been organized by Lawrie Garland, Christian Petersen and Paul Stillman, a North Midlands Group by Michael Clarke, a Central Midlands Group by Peter Jepson (previously run by John & Nellie Steadman), a Cotswolds Group by Rahel Bridgen and Tim Bates, a North-West Group by Stephen and Fay Howard, and a North-East Group by Bryan Spark.

[7]**Nikon Historical Society:** The Nikon Historical Society is based in the U.S. and has a worldwide membership. *The Nikon Journal*, published four times a year, concentrates on the history of Japanese photo equipment from the perspective of the Nikon Camera Company. It was founded by Robert Rotoloni.

[8]**Robin Williamson:** Robin Williamson first sprang to fame in the late 'sixties as the lead singer, virtuoso instrumentalist and co-founder of The Incredible String Band. He influenced a generation of musicians as diverse as John Lennon, Bob Dylan, Robert Plant and the Eurythmics. *"Part poet, part musician, part storyteller, part cultural guardian, he is the consummate performer, at once captivating in his artistry, delightful in his wit..."* – San Diego Times

[9]**Mari Llwyd:** Mari Llwyd is a grey mare's skull that is carried around with a burning candle mounted inside. Robin Williamson extended this poem into a song which appears on his CD *The Island of the Strong Door* (The Music Corporation TMC 9504).

[10]**Terence Donovan:** Terence Donovan (14 September 1936 – 22 November 1996) was an English photographer and film director, best remembered for his fashion photography of the 1960s. He came to particular prominence in the 1960s as part of the now famous era of 'Swinging London'. Associated at the time with David Bailey and Brian Duffy, these three English photographers revolutionised the world of magazine and newspaper photography. He is considered to be one of this country's greatest photographers.

[11]**Shogun:** a shogun was a hereditary commander-in-chief in feudal Japan. Because of the military power concentrated in his hands and the consequent weakness of the nominal head of state (the Mikado or Emperor), the shogun was generally the real ruler of the country until feudalism was abolished in 1867.

PHOTOGRAPHERS & PHOTOGRAPHIC WRITERS

Scott Andrews:
The celebrated former Nikon U.S.A. technical troubleshooter Scott Andrews worked for a number of years for Nikon Professional Services in Washington, DC. He has also worked with the White House Press and *National Geographic* as well as being directly involved in assisting NASA to record the evolving history of the International Space Station. Since the advent of the Space Shuttle Programme, he has recorded many launches using remote camera techniques.

Heather Angel:
(see page 12)

John Archer-Thomson:
Respected photographer and author John Archer-Thomson was the former Senior Assistant Director of Dale Fort Field Centre, a marine and coastal ecology Centre run by the Field Studies Council. He is now a freelance coastal ecologist, writer and photographer. His recent publication *Photographing Pembrokeshire* was co-written with his wife Sally.

Jim Brandenburg:
The legendary environmentalist, nature photographer and filmmaker Jim Brandenburg travelled the globe as a photographer with *National Geographic* magazine for over three decades. He has been published in numerous national and international publications including the *New York Times, Life, Time, Audubon, Smithsonian, Natural History, GEO, Modern Maturity, BBC Wildlife, Outdoor Photographer, National Wildlife* and *Outside*. He has received a multitude of prestigious national and international honours for his work including the the Lifetime Achievement Award by the North American Nature Photographers Association (NANPA), as well as the World Achievement Award from the United Nations Environmental Programme in Stockholm, Sweden.

Tami Bahat:
Tami Bahat is an award-winning fine art photographer whose passion lies in moulding the obvious into the extraordinary. Tami is one of an elite group of emerging Los Angeles photographers and her photography has been featured in numerous publications, as well as in gallery exhibitions across America and Europe. Her treatment of the photographic medium is almost mythic and she deals eloquently with light and shade, weaving life and movement into the image she wants to communicate to the viewer.

Sue Bishop: Sue Bishop specialises in flower and landscape photography. Her aim is to create an image that is more than a mere record of its subject and her compositions are a celebration of colour, light and form, sometimes going beyond reality so that they become impressionistic or abstract. Flower photography is a particular passion, and Sue has written two books on the subject, *Photographing Flowers and Digital Flower Photography*. *Color, Light & Composition*, published in January 2010, is illustrated with both landscape and flower images.

Michael Bright:
Michael Bright worked as executive producer with the BBC Natural History Unit for a number of years. He was a recipient of the prestigious Prix Italia for the programme *Men, Nations and Whales: will the bloody story ever end?* and is the author of over 100 books on natural history, natural sciences, conservation and the environment for BBC Books, *Reader's Digest,* Dorling Kindersley, *National Geographic,* Raintree, Quarto, Franklin Watts, the Natural History Museum, and the Smithsonian, to name but a few. Alongside radio and film work, Michael has also written articles for *BBC Wildlife, BBC Focus, New Scientist, World Medicine* as well as *Nikon Owner* magazine.

Julian Calder:
Julian Calder is an internationally renowned photographer, who has photographed numerous stories and assignments for leading national and international magazines. He specialises in portraits and his work has been published around the world and exhibited at the National Portrait Gallery, London. Julian's celebrated portrait of HM The Queen, which is on the cover of *Keepers: The Ancient Offices of Britain* (published in 2013) is now in The Scottish National Portrait Gallery. His latest book, *The Queen's Birthday Parade: Trooping of the Colour* was published in June 2015.

David duChemin:
David duChemin is a world and humanitarian assignment photographer, best-selling author, digital publisher and international workshop leader whose nomadic and adventurous life fuels his photography and the compelling images he has taken in all seven continents. When on assignment David creates powerful pictures that convey the hope and dignity of children, the vulnerable and oppressed, for the international NGO community. David is the founder and Chief Executive Nomad of Craft & Vision, Editor in Chief of *PHOTOGRAPH* magazine, and a contributing columnist to *PHOTOLIFE*.

Michael Doven:
(see page 48)

Graham Eaton:
Graham Eaton is a multi-award winning photographer, who specialises in wildlife and landscape photography. A consultant geologist by profession, Graham has travelled from Alaska to Azerbaijan and from Norway to the Red Sea in search of photographic opportunities. His work has been widely published, and he has been awarded in many National and International Photography competitions such as The British Wildlife Photography Awards, The Wildlife Photographer of the Year, and The Landscape Photographer of the Year. Graham photographs wildlife within the landscape, seeking 'alternative' perspectives, capturing mood, movement and atmosphere in a 'living' landscape image.

Richard Edlund:
Richard Edlund is a multi-Academy Award-winning U.S. special effects cinematographer. He was first cameraman at the embryonic Industrial Light & Magic on the production of *Star Wars* for which he shared an Academy Award. He worked on *Battlestar Galactica* and was invited by George Lucas to work on *The Empire Strikes Back*, resulting in a second Academy Award. Edlund also worked on *Raiders of the Lost Ark* and *Poltergeist* and many other distinguished productions. He set up his own effects company, Boss Films, one of the first traditional effects houses that successfully transitioned from 'tangible world' visual effects to CGI.

Michael Eleftheriades:
(see page 60)

Robert Falconer:
Based in Vancouver, Canada, Robert Falconer is a versatile communications professional, a multi-disciplinary writer, content producer and photographer. He began his career penning scripts for television series such as *Star Trek: The Next Generation* and its subsequent spin-offs. More recently he has applied his skills to the sectors of business, media, and journalism, where he has worked with a variety of organisations, including *Metro News* and *National Geographic* channel. In addition to being a long-time Nikon shooter and devotee, Robert is also a Fujifilm X-Photographer.

Bruce Fleming:
Bruce Fleming is a British fine art photographer who is notable for his pop art portraits of the 1960s and 1970s. He is perhaps best known for his photography of the Hollies, The Dave Clark Five, Lulu, the Animals and Jimi Hendrix, whose picture he took many times. He produced the image for the Jimi Hendrix Experience's album cover *Are You Experienced* in 1967, which was taken in the Royal Botanic Gardens in Kew.

Graham Hancock & Santha Faiia:
Graham Hancock's books have sold more than five million copies worldwide and have been translated into 27 languages. His public lectures and two major TV series *Quest For The Lost Civilisation* and *Flooded Kingdoms of the Ice Age* have put his ideas before audiences of tens of millions. Graham's wife, Santha Faiia is a professional photographer specialising in ancient cultures and monuments. Her work has been published around the world in major newspapers and magazines. Her latest work can be seen in the 32 pages of colour photographs that she has contributed to *Magicians of the Gods*, Graham Hancock's latest work.

Paul Joynson-Hicks:
Paul Joynson-Hicks is a professional photographer based on Tanzania's east coast. At the heart of Paul's photography is his exuberant passion for Africa, where he has lived and worked for 14 years, and this is reflected in his books which celebrate in photographs the drama of Tanzania, Uganda and the South Luangwa Valley in Zambia. Paul Joynson-Hicks has also set up a number of charitable organisations to assist some of the poorest people in the world.

Felix Kunze:
Felix Kunze is a portraiture photographer who was born in East Berlin and grew up in Sussex, England. He is now based in New York City but travels for projects around the globe. As well as some photo assisting for Annie Leibovitz in

New York and Mario Testino in London, he shoots assignments for agencies such as Getty Images, WireImage, the Redferns Music Library, Getty Travel and others, including celebrity portraits at Contour photos.

Neil Lucas:
(see page 98)

Philip Makanna:
Philip Makanna has been called the 'world's greatest aviation photographer', pursuing his childhood dream to photograph classic WWI and WWII aircraft. The first *GHOSTS* calendar comprised of Makanna's genre-defining aerial photography and was published by Philip and his wife Jeanie in 1980. Their 2015 calendar marked the 35th edition of the now world-renowned *GHOSTS* calendar. Makanna regularly makes trips to document the great collections of airplanes in the U.K., New Zealand, and Australia and throughout the U.S.A..

Mike Maloney OBE:
(see page 108)

Sir Simon Marsden:
(see page 114)

Chris Martin:
As an accomplished mountaineer and skier, Chris Martin has led and participated in expeditions across the globe, particularly throughout the Himalaya regions, Europe, North America and Alaska. His photographic work focuses on capturing the beauty of the more remote places on the planet and the cultures who inhabit them. He has used his writing and photographs in many U.K. publications to highlight how a way of life for these indigenous cultures, which had existed for thousands of years, are now in the process of dramatic and irreversible change.

Patrick McMullan:
Patrick McMullan is one of the premier photographers of New York City nightlife. Born in New York and raised on Long Island, McMullan first started taking pictures of society gatherings while frequenting Studio 54 as a student. Practically a social documentarian, McMullan's work chronicles the history of New York celebrities over the past three decades, including the intermingling of stars from the worlds of fashion and art.

Joe McNally:
(see page 122)

Moose Peterson:
(see page 140)

Ken Regan:
The late Ken Regan's photographic work covered the World Series, Super Bowl, the Olympics, heavyweight championship fights, hockey, basketball, tennis, auto racing and other professional sports for *Time, Sports Illustrated, Life* and *Newsweek*. Ken photographed sports legends such as Muhammad Ali and Mike Tyson as well as some of the most renowned musicians in Rock & Roll, such as the Beatles on their first visit to the United States in 1964.

Martin Shann:
From 1996 until December 2005, Martin Shann was Head of Production Technology for Aardman Animations, and until he retired their Media Methologist and their Research and Discovery Peripatetic Image Scientist. Martin had both the vision and the innovative imagination needed to create and utilise photographic digital systems which themselves have technically accelerated and advanced the technology behind clay animation.

Brian Slater:
Brian Slater is a stunning dance and theatre photographer who has worked very closely with Northern Ballet for a number of years. Motion is an unbelievably difficult area to capture proficiently, but his work catches the essence of movement and form with a rare grace and beauty. A Nikon user for all of his career, he now photographs all styles of dance: Ballet, Contemporary, Hip-hop etc., as well as documenting the U.K. youth dance culture. In 2013 his exhibition Youth Dance Captured was very well-received at The Leeds Gallery.

David Suchet CBE:
(see page 156)

Mark Tillie:
Mark Tillie is a highly respected, award-winning photographer. A selection of his work is in The National Portrait Gallery and he has won awards from The Association of Photographers and The John Kobal Portrait Awards. Mark also worked as the stills photographer in over thirty feature films including the Oscar nominated *Gosford Park, Moon, Mrs. Brown, The Wings of the Dove, The Englishman Who Went Up a Hill but Came Down a Mountain* and *Shine*.

Simon Weir:
Based in London, Simon Weir specialises in photographing live performance (particularly classical music), contextual portraiture, wildlife and nature. He often uses specially prepared silent and remote controlled cameras for his images of live performances. He has a lifelong love of black & white imagery and infra-red photography; using specially modified cameras he is able to capture scenes entirely composed of invisible infra-red light, producing an alternative view of reality: beyond visible light.

Chris Weston:
(see page 168)

Andrew Main Wilson:
(see page 196)

Richard Young:
(see page 202)

THE PHOTOGRAPHS

Front cover by Michael Eleftheriades, Page 2 by Konstantin Kochkin, Pages 4 & 7 by Mike Eleftheriades, Page 11 Illustration of shop front by Norman McLynchy, Page 12 Heather Angel by Natalie Johnson, Page 15 Shop front by Tony Hurst, Page 16 Nigel Atherton - *Amateur Photographer*/ Time Inc. (UK) Ltd, Pages 19-25 + 27 by Konstantin Kochkin, Page 26 Nikon FM3A by Simon Stafford, Page 28 Michael Bond by Anthony Barwell, Pages 31 & 32 Brass plate & 15mm UV-Nikkor by Tony Hurst, Page 34 Garry Coward-Williams by Michael Topham, Page 37 Julia Margaret Cameron © Julia Margaret Cameron Trust www.dimbola.co.uk, Page 38 Louis Daguerre by Christie's www.christies.com/cameras, Page 39 The girl in the striped dress by Fred Pegram - Kodak advert, Page 40 Calypso/Nikkor II by Tony Hurst, Page 42 Damien Demolder by Catrina Demolder, Page 45 Gray Levett Glastonbury Tor by Michael Spiller, Page 46 Gray on Bournemouth Beach by Thomas Levett, Page 47 Gray Levett's Nikon F by Tony Hurst, Page 48 Michael Doven by Denice Duff, Page 52 Left: Masahiko Fuketa - photographer unknown, Page 52 Right David Douglas Duncan by Ray Fisher, Page 53 Hansa Canon by Tony Hurst, Page 54 Interior of Nikon factory - photographerr unknown, Page 56 Nikon SP black + S-36 c/w 5cm f/1.1 Nikkor by Tony Hurst, Page 57 Nikon S3M + S-36 motor drive by Tony Hurst, Page 59 Nikon F + 5cm f/2 Nikkor by Tony Hurst, Page 60 Michael Eleftheriades by Konstantin Kochkin, Page 64 N. Hartle Photographic by Grahame Austin Kitchenshams Ltd, Page 65 Gray at KJP by Kit Walker, Page 66 Gray at Leslie S. Miller by Kit Walker, Page 67 Keith Emerson by Gray Levett, Page 67 The Nice poster - artist unknown, Page 67 bottom left Rod Stewart and The Soul Agents - photographer unknown, Page 68 Left Gray Levett & Robin Williamson by Georgianna Lane, Page 68 Right 'U' poster by Janet Williamson, Page 69 Kate Bush by Trinity Mirror/Mirrorpix/Alamy Stock Photo, Page 69 Glen Row by Janet Williamson, Page 70 Gray Levett & Forrest J Ackerman by Kit Walker, Page 72 Gray Levett - photographer unknown, Page 72 Art Garfunkel, Gray & Nicky Hopkins by Stephen Mallaby, Page 74 John Krish - photographer unknown, Page 77 Sir Winston Churchill © Imperial War Museum, Pages 78 & 79 Churton Street - photographer unknown, Page 80 Thomas Cubitt by Simon Stafford, Page 84 Stanley Kubrick by Manuel Harlan, Page 87 GoW at Susie Levett's flat by Gray Levett, Page 88 White's Barbers by Gray Levett, Page 90 Daniel Lezano by Jo Lezano, Page 93 Brass bell by Simon Stafford, Page 95 GoW painting by Kridon Panteli, Page 96 Brass light switches by Konstantin Kochkin, Page 97 Door Bell, telephone by Simon Stafford, Wall Calendar by Konstantin Kochkin, Page 98 Neil Lucas by Keith Brust, Page 101 Nikkor F by Tony Hurst, Page 103 Nikon F3 Lapita by Tony Hurst, Page 104 GoW sign by Michael Eleftheriades, Page 105 Christmas Shop - photographer unknown, Page 106 GoW flag by Simon Stafford, Page 107 GoW carrier bag by Tony Hurst, Page 108 Mike Maloney OBE - photographer unknown, Page 111, 112, 113 Uri Zakay by Felix Kunze, Page 114 Sir Simon Marsden by Cassie Marsden, Page 117 Gray Levett by Felix Kunze, Pages 118, 119, 120 by Konstantin Kochkin, Page 122 Joe McNally by Annie Cahill, Page 129 *Nikon Owner* covers by Jesse Wilson, Page 130 Saint Hill Manor by Golden Era Productions, Page 131 Institute of Directors by © IoD, Page 132 Tristan Oliver by Will Reid, Page 135 Book cover by Robert Rotoloni, Page 136 Instruction manuals by Tony Hurst, Page 137 Vintage Nikon Rangefinder cabinet by Konstantin Kochkin, Pages 138 & 139 Nippon Kogaku Room by Stefano Barozzi, Page 140 Moose Peterson by Scott Kelby, Page 144 Awards by Tony Hurst, Becky Danese, Simon Stafford, Page 145 Porecelain Plate by Felix Kunze, Pages 146 & 147 by Tony Hurst, Page 148 Simon Stafford by Holly Stafford, Page 152 The College of Arms by Konstantin Kochkin, Page 153 Coat of Arms by Simon Stafford, Page 155 Robert Noel by Julian Calder, Page 156 David Suchet by Simon Stafford, Page 160 GoW brolly by Tony Hurst, Page 162 Catalogue & instruction books by Tony Hurst, Page 163 Fribourg & Treyer photographer unknown, Page 164 GoW Christmas Catalogue Candle by Tony Hurst, Page 165 Robin Williamson photographer unknown, Pages 166 & 167 GoW paperweight by Tony Hurst, Page 168 Chris Weston by Monique By Monique Brignoni, Pages 172-195 Nikon equipment by Tony Hurst, Page 196 Andrew Main Wilson by Felix Kunze, Page 200 Jim Brandenburg - photographer unknown, Page 200 (GoW brass) and 201 by Mike Eleftheriades, 202 Richard Young by Lorenzo Agius, Author photograph of Gillian Greenwood by Stephanie Rushton